CAREER ROULETTE

NAVIGATING THE CHAOTIC JOURNEY OF MODERN ADULTING

J.T. PAIGE

Copyright © 2024 by J.T. Paige

All rights reserved.

No portion of this book may be reproduced in any form without written permission from the publisher or author, except as permitted by U.S. copyright law.

This publication is designed to provide accurate and authoritative information in regard to the subject matter covered. It is sold with the understanding that neither the author nor the publisher is engaged in rendering legal, investment, accounting, or other professional services. While the publisher and author have used their best efforts in preparing this book, they make no representations or warranties with respect to the accuracy or completeness of the contents of this book and specifically disclaim any implied warranties of merchantability or fitness for a particular purpose. No warranty may be created or extended by sales representatives or written sales materials. The advice and strategies contained herein may not be suitable for your situation. You should consult with a professional when appropriate. Neither the publisher nor the author shall be liable for any loss of profit or any other commercial damages, including but not limited to special, incidental, consequential, personal, or other damages.

First edition 2024

ISBN: 979-8328274968 (paperback), IBSN: 979-8328536158 (hardcover), ASIN: B0D6VHS5RJ (ebook)

Contact: jt.publishing4@gmail.com

CONTENTS

Introduction	7
1. THE PARALYSIS BY ANALYSIS SYNDROME	11
1.1 The Myth of the Perfect Choice	11
1.2 Overcoming the Fear of the Wrong Turn	13
1.3 Analysis Paralysis: Recognizing the Symptoms	16
1.4 The Decision-Making Toolkit for the Indecisive	21
1.5 Action over Perfection: A Case for "Good Enough"	24
2. THE DIGITAL DILEMMA AND ITS DESIDERATUM	27
2.1 Digital Literacy: A Non-Negotiable Skill	27
2.2 Social Media: The Double-Edged Sword	29
2.3 Online Presence and Personal Branding 101	31
2.4 Cybersecurity for Beginners: Safeguarding Your Digital Footprint	34
2.5 From Digital Consumer to Creator: Making the Leap	37
3. BUDGET LIKE A BAD B*TCH	41
3.1 Understanding Your Money Mindset	41
3.2 The Art of Budgeting When You Hate Numbers	43
3.3 Smart Saving Strategies for Future Flexibility	47
3.4 Demystifying Student Loans and Debt	49
3.5 Investing in Yourself: Skills Over Stocks	52
4. THE ENTREPRENEURIAL SPIRIT UNLEASHED	57
4.1 The Side Hustle Starter Pack	57
4.2 Bootstrap Your Business: Low-Cost Startup Strategies	60
4.3 From Passion Project to Profit: The How-To	61
4.4 Navigating Failures and Setbacks as a Young Entrepreneur	64
4.5 The Gig Economy: Making It Work for You	66

5. **MARKETABLE SKILLS BEYOND THE DEGREE** — 70
   - 5.1 Digital Marketing: What Everyone Should Know — 70
   - 5.2 Coding for the Non-Techie: Why It Matters — 73
   - 5.3 Public Speaking and Persuasion in the Digital Age — 76
   - 5.4 The Power of Networking: Beyond the Business Card — 79
   - 5.5 Creative Problem-Solving and Innovation — 82

6. **THE SELF-CARE CAREERIST** — 87
   - 6.1 Work-Life Balance: Myths, Realities, and Strategies — 87
   - 6.2 Mental Health in the Workplace: Breaking the Taboo — 90
   - 6.3 The Burnout Generation: Signs, Symptoms, and Solutions — 92
   - 6.4 Mindfulness and Productivity: A Symbiotic Relationship — 95
   - 6.5 Saying No: The Ultimate Career and Life Skill — 97

7. **ALTERNATIVE EDUCATION AND CAREER PATHS** — 101
   - 7.1 Vocational Training and Apprenticeships: The Unsung Heroes — 101
   - 7.2 Online Learning Platforms: Tailoring Education to Your Needs — 103
   - 7.3 The Case for Gap Years: Pros, Cons, and Possibilities — 105
   - 7.4 Breaking Into Tech Without a Tech Degree — 108
   - 7.5 Crafting a Career in the Creative Industries — 110

8. **THE GLOBAL CAREER ADVENTURE** — 114
   - 8.1 Teaching English Abroad: More Than a Gap Year — 114
   - 8.2 Remote Work and Digital Nomadism: Is It for You? — 117
   - 8.3 International Internships: A Stepping Stone to Global Careers — 120

8.4 Volunteering as Career Development: Building Skills While Giving Back	121
8.5 Cultural Competence in the Global Job Market	123
9. PREPARING FOR TOMORROW'S JOB MARKET TODAY	125
9.1 Emerging Industries and Where to Find Them	125
9.2 The Role of Artificial Intelligence in Future Careers	127
9.3 Sustainability and Green Jobs: The Next Big Thing	128
9.4 Lifelong Learning: Keeping Skills Sharp in a Fast-Paced World	130
9.5 Creating Your Own Opportunities: The Ultimate Career Hack	131
Conclusion	133
Spread the Love: Leave a Review	135
Bibliography	139

INTRODUCTION

Welcome to the unpredictable world of career exploration, where uncertainty is the only guarantee and the path to success is more like a game of roulette than a straight line. Sure, there are a few rare souls who map out their lives on a spreadsheet from a young age—and an even rarer few who actually stick to it! But even their seemingly smooth, EV-powered journey has its bumps and breakdowns—and that's okay! For most of us, careers shift and evolve, and it's this unpredictability that makes the journey both exhilarating and a little terrifying.

In an ever-changing world where it's the norm to juggle day jobs with e-learning, side hustles, and side pieces (jk, unless that's your thing) and where increasingly intense self-care regimens are encouraged, staying focused is getting even more challenging!

It takes more time than you think to find that dream job, and that dream job may not be dependable; a fair warning- they can be fleeting! You may think you've found that sweet sugar daddy of a job that was meant to give you a happy security blanket for life, then POW! It reveals that it was just a heartless f*ckboy all along, kicking you out of his apartment after promising you the world (Okay, I might have been trauma-dumping there, but you get what I mean!).

Sounds like a hot mess, right? That's because it very often is, and that's totally normal. I'm here to guide you through this wild ride of job hunting, soul searching, and, let's be real, occasional panic Googling at 2 AM. My mission? To arm you with high-speed internet GPS as we navigate the sh*tstorm that is modern adulting and career planning. I'm here to throw out the rulebook, mix in some laughs, and maybe, just maybe, help us all figure out what in the world we're doing.

This book is my vulgar love letter to all you overwhelmed young (or old) adults out there staring down the barrel of "WTF do I do next?" I've been there, and I know that right now you're all sick of the B.S. cliche advice you get from your relative you see once a year or from the influencer who's taking artistic photos of lip gloss next to a collagen rose latte. Some of their advice might be legit, but some may not be, so I'm here to be real with you and find the golden nuggets of truth in the giant heaping pile of cr*p advice.

In this book, we'll cover everything from zig-zagging through non-traditional career paths to becoming digital ninjas to keeping the ego-devouring "low balance" notifications out of your inbox. I know firsthand how daunting this all can be, so I'm providing helpful exercises and worksheets so we can be proactive! If I didn't, it'd be like gifting you a dead vibrator without a charger (not helpful!).

This is real and unfiltered advice from a gal who has been

INTRODUCTION

THROUGH IT. I truly want to pay it forward and give you the necessary tools. Seriously, I am HERE for you on this journey. Whether you're a recent graduate, a seasoned professional, or somewhere in between, this book is your guide to navigating the twists and turns of finding your path in a world where the only constant is change. Get ready for a wild ride filled with laughter, insight, and the occasional swear word – because when it comes to careers, sometimes you just have to roll with the punches, close your eyes, and spin that wheel. Welcome to Career Roulette – let the games begin!

[1]
THE PARALYSIS BY ANALYSIS SYNDROME

1.1 THE MYTH OF THE PERFECT CHOICE

From the moment we begin our education, we're asked by teachers, peers, family, and friends- "What do you want to be when you grow up?" It's aimed to help us become motivated for our futures, but when you think about it- it's actually f*cking hilarious to consider that a first grader knows what their future will be. I was looking through my elementary school portfolios the other day, and each year, I had a new goal. In kindergarten, I wanted to be a princess (after watching The Crown, I now know that goal is way overrated. Thanks adulthood, another dream CRUSHED). In first grade, I wanted to be a librarian (better). In second grade, this was the most realistic- a "starving artist!" (Aim big, little one!)

Now, at 30 years old, I STILL don't know if what I am doing is what I'll do for the rest of my life, nor do I know if it's what I SHOULD be doing for the rest of my life. But you know what? The best part of maturing is accepting that! Seriously. If you relax and embrace the fact that we're all playing constant games of roulette with our careers, you'll feel a sense of relief.

There are always going to be naysayers when it comes to this logic. Once the "What do you want to be?" questions start, the prying questions just keep getting more detailed as life goes on. "What's your plan?" "What are you going to major in?" "Where do you see yourself in ten years?" "Are you planning on marrying your prom date?" WHAT?!

Even if you DO know what you want at a young age, there are these OTHER pressures to choose what OTHER PEOPLE think is best for you! The secret is to continue and believe that your future is for you and nobody else to decide. There will be so many people along the way who will question you and their motives don't always have the best intentions. The secret is to have confidence and keep putting in the work. Don't listen to family and peers who pressure you into following their idea of success.

There is no single dream job for anybody. Some may decide to settle in one career because they become comfortable and feel a sense of security, which is fine. However, it is quite natural to have multiple careers and multiple dreams! Martha Stewart was a model and a stockbroker before she became the goddess of homemaking (she also made the cover of Sports Illustrated in 2023 at 81-QUEEN!). Vera Wang was a figure skater before she became a fashion designer. Sarah Blakely sold fax machines before she became the founder of Spanx and reshaped fashion (literally).

The search for the mythical "dream job" never ends because it is a myth! You will, quite naturally, always be searching for what is next, and that is perfectly healthy.

Don't wait around for the perfect dream job to fall into your lap, and don't wait for the perfect opportunity to make a move. That perfect opportunity does not exist, so make the moves that feel right to you today.

1.2 OVERCOMING THE FEAR OF THE WRONG TURN

Atychiphobia, the disease that's certain to keep you from reaching your goals. No, it's not a taboo venereal disease; it's a term for the fear of failure. It's not an official medical term. However, it is psychologically real and bound to keep you from success. Fear is sure to stifle creativity, productivity, and experimentation. Fear leads to procrastination, and procrastination leads to, well... nothing.

You can only succeed at something if you try. Yes, you will likely fail the first time you try, but that's okay. Failure, in a way, is actually success. It means that you tried and that you were able to learn something from your mistakes. The Japanese have a word for this methodology. It's called *kaizen*. Kaizen, literally translated, means "good change." It's conscientious improvement, learning little by little by trying again and again and learning from mistakes.

Think of a toddler learning how to walk. They don't just stand up and suddenly start strutting around the house flawlessly like Tyra Banks. No, they first try to stand, and they fall over on their heinies, over and over. Next, they learn they can use a sofa for support. They let go, and they fall again. Finally, they start stumbling across the carpet like a divorcee who just had a crazy night at Margaritaville, and again- they fall. The constant failure doesn't bother them (the toddlers, not the divorcees. The divorcees may be feeling a bit bothered the next morning) because they (the toddlers) lack the fragile egos of adults, and by instinct, they KNOW they are capable of walking. If only all of us still had that tenacity, that lack of self-doubt.

There are plenty of exceptional examples of resilience through failures. Walt Disney is a prime example. He was a "failed" cartoonist who was laughed out of the banks when he asked for loans, and his first company went bankrupt. Did he let that stop him? No. He had confidence in his vision and knew that if he just kept trying, he would eventually succeed. Look at the empire he built, which is now a multi-billion dollar legacy.

Thomas Edison famously said, "I have not failed. I've just found 10,000 ways that won't work." What an incredible sense of self-assurance. Edison was known for his monumental inventions, including the lightbulb and the phonograph (the first device to record and playback sound). However, people don't know that he also successfully invented gadgets that "did not work." For instance, he sold electric pens that produced very messy handwriting and talking dolls with "ghastly voices" (That screams horror movie- yikes!). If Thomas Edison had given up after any of his many inventions that didn't sell, he wouldn't have gifted society with his more notable inventions that inspired the technology we have today.

Reminding ourselves of the accomplishments of those who failed is one of many practices that will help us overcome our own fears of failure. Practicing failure is another way to overcome it. Psychologists suggest trying something new as a way to gain confidence. It doesn't have to be something major. It could be as simple

THE PARALYSIS BY ANALYSIS SYNDROME

as a fun new hobby like learning the ukulele, speaking a new language, or knitting a scarf. Learning new skills takes time, and it builds our courage. I dare you to **try something new this week**. Not only will it help you to overcome the fear of failure, but it'll also help you to practice mindfulness, which is an integral part of maintaining life balance (which we'll cover in another chapter).

Journaling can also help overcome hurdles. I'm more of an introvert myself, so whenever I'm struggling mentally, I write everything down on paper, and suddenly, my thoughts become clearer, and the answers to my burning questions pour out onto the paper. Creative guides often suggest writing three pages each morning. It may seem daunting, but even if you begin by writing "I have nothing to write about" over and over, you'll suddenly have something to write about and vomit all your thoughts onto the page.

I dare you to **try something new this week**, and then **write what you learned from your mistakes** each time you try. Then, **TRY AGAIN**. I triple-dog dare you (yup, that's right, now you have no choice).

Remember, "With no risk, there is no reward." You don't get rewarded for taking the easy road. Also, "There is no failure, only feedback." I can spew out these corny quotes all day, but I think you get my drift by now. It's up to you to get out of your comfort zone and escape your negative thoughts. You can only win career roulette if you're bold enough to spin the wheel!

If you're reading this and you STILL have Negative Nancy in your head telling you that these lessons don't apply to you, know that she is wrong! And also, know that it's totally possible to get rid of her and reframe your mind. Cognitive Behavioral Therapy

(CBT) is proven to be an effective way to change how you speak to yourself and use solution-based imagery to maintain a positive mindset. Below are books and links for you to explore further.

- *Cognitive Behavioral Theory Made Simple* by Seth J. Gillihan
- *Cognitive Behavior Therapy: Basics and Beyond* by Judith S. Beck
- healthline.com/health/cognitive-behavioral-therapy

I think I've made my point about the importance of letting yourself fail, so let's review your challenges this week:

1. Jot down a few successful people who overcame failure. Let them be your muses and your inspiration whenever your inner voice tries to tell you that you can't do something.
2. TRY SOMETHING NEW!
3. Journal what you learned from your failures.
4. Reshape your mind with Cognitive Behavioral Therapy.

1.3 ANALYSIS PARALYSIS: RECOGNIZING THE SYMPTOMS

You've just finished your tasks for the night after a long day of work, and it's finally ME-TIME! Ah yes. The best time of the night when you can unwind and do whatever the f*ck you want. You put on your baggy sweats and cozy socks, grab your cat (even if it's against their will) and snuggle up on the couch. Then, suddenly, an overwhelming feeling of indecision overwhelms you. You sort through all the apps: Hulu, Netflix, Paramount, Max, Peacock, Disney, Prime. You sort out your favorites from each, and then you start analyzing the f*ck out of what you SHOULD be watching. Should you watch something educational? Should you watch that movie your co-worker suggested out of comradery? Should you get back to your guilty pleasure trash reality TV show? Or should you watch the latest Oscar nominations so you feel more in tune with the cinephiles? Suddenly, a simple night of unwinding has you all wound up, and before you know it, you've spent over an HOUR thinking about what to turn on! So much for relaxation.

Sure, with all the content and options out there, it's tough to find something to watch, but if this overanalysis leading to indecision is a pattern you notice in that dirty mind of yours, you may be a victim of "analysis paralysis."

Analysis paralysis is the inability to make a decision due to chronic overthinking. It makes every little decision difficult. Picking restaurants, deciding what to wear, and writing emails. These all take an excruciating, exhausting amount of self-judgment and overanalysis, so how the HELL are you supposed to make big life decisions? Well, most people that follow this pattern just DON'T! Yes, they just drop the ball and stay on a rusting conveyor belt to nowhere. Even if they're unhappy with their job, lifestyle, or relationship, they do nothing about it because of the negative impact of *decision fatigue*.

It's impossible to have the energy to move forward with a decision when making the decision has you panting breathless on the floor, begging for a B-12 shot straight in the ass just so you can keep your eyes open (okay, that was drastic, but you get me, right?). This is why analysis paralysis leads to missed opportunities and a significant slump in creativity. How can you have an open mind when it's clogged up with so many indecisive barriers? You can't! That's why it is so important to recognize if you suffer from analysis paralysis and get the help you need so you can overcome it and make confident decisions.

If you've read to this point and are still unsure whether you have these tendencies, there are several free psychological assessments available online.

- www.psychologytoday.com/us/tests- Test everything from your self-esteem to your sexual openness and everything in between.
- www.screening.mhanational.org/screening-tools/ - Answer questions to test different aspects of your mental health (depression, anxiety, ADHD, etc.)

***Disclaimer: These ~3 minute online tests are not meant to diagnose any mental health conditions; that's a job for the doctor, not the internet, but they can help you understand why you may think or act the way you do.

The first step in overcoming analysis paralysis is knowing the root causes. Often, the broad causes are anxiety, depression, and low self-esteem. So, if you knowingly suffer from any of the above, there's a higher chance that you can easily identify a time you held yourself from valuable opportunities due to indecision.

Treating the root causes through meditation, exercise, and therapy will always help. However, it is equally important to assess the more immediate causes of analysis paralysis. **Know your triggers!**

THE PARALYSIS BY ANALYSIS SYNDROME

For our first exercise, take a deep breath, open a notebook or laptop, and **write down the types decisions that overwhelm you**. Ask yourself what about these decisions makes them problematic. Is it the associated risks? Is it social pressure? Fear of change?

Next, **identify how your body responds** to analysis paralysis. When you are overwhelmed, can you feel your heart rate increase? Do you have difficulty sleeping? Do your thoughts ruminate (in other words, do the negative overanalytical thoughts in your head never shut the f*ck up?)? Recognizing the symptoms is essential, so you know when it's time to stop and take a breather.

Self-awareness is crucial because it lets you know when it's time to **create distance**. How do you create distance? As always, meditating and breathing slowly will help. If you can meditate, it is so- and I cannot stress this enough- f*cking helpful. Not everyone can meditate easily. Some think it's a bunch of woo-woo. I know, I struggled with that mentality myself, so I find other ways to create space. Sometimes, I go for walks (being sure to be mindful and not look at my cell phone). Other times, I find stillness somewhere in nature (on a rooftop or in a quiet room for my urban readers). Exercise also helps. Do whatever you need to do to step away mentally, even if just for a moment. If you're at work and can't actually step away when you're overwhelmed, take a deep breath and move on to a more manageable task before returning to the difficult one. Creating space for that overwhelming task will absolutely make it easier.

If you have the time and opportunity, another beneficial tool is TALKING. **Talk to someone**. Talk to a family member, a colleague, a therapist, a wise woman on the bus who is willing to lend an ear.

Tell them about the decision you're trying to make and explain why it's complicated. Just talking about it will help you see the answers more clearly and help you notice when you're being over-analytical. And if you're lucky, you might even get some really great advice from the person you're talking to! (**Disclaimer: Since this is a no B.S. guide, I do have to acknowledge that some friends give really terrible advice, and the "wise" woman from the bus may turn out to just be batsh*t crazy**. BUT it's still healthy to talk it out!).

If you're going to talk to someone, perhaps the best person to talk to is someone who has decision-making skills that you respect. Is there someone whose ability to make quick, confident decisions inspires you? **Write down their names. Write about the qualities in those people that make you respect them**, and when you get the opportunity, **ask them for advice**! Ask them how they avoid the constant "what-ifs." Ask them how they're able to make quicker decisions. Do they meditate? Do they simply trust their intuition and expertise? Take note and try to use their tactics in your own everyday decisions.

Everyone loves a list, so here's a list of what you can do for yourself to overcome analysis paralysis:

1. Self-Assessments: Take an online test to decipher whether you suffer from chronic indecision.
2. Know the Symptoms: Recognize your triggers and your symptoms.
3. Create Space: Take a breather when you notice you're falling into a deep, bottomless pit of "WTF DO I DO?!".

THE PARALYSIS BY ANALYSIS SYNDROME

Step away for a moment if you can, or move on to a more manageable task and revisit.
4. Talk It Out: Talk to someone you trust about your inability to make a decision.
5. Ask for Advice: Jot down the names of people with decision-making skills you respect and ask them for tips.

1.4 THE DECISION-MAKING TOOLKIT FOR THE INDECISIVE

So, we've spoken a lot about the psychology behind fear and indecision. Now, it's time to talk about the tools you can use to overcome indecision regarding business. Even if you don't feel like you're an indecisive person and don't think you need more tools, you should read this because these are beneficial in other ways.

First, let's talk about SWOT analysis (See? I told you this would be beneficial! Now you'll know WTF colleagues are talking about when they use this term at work or on LinkedIn). SWOT analysis is a fancy pants corporate way of listing pros and cons due to "internal and external factors." Here's an example of a SWOT Analysis Template Spreadsheet so you can follow along. SWOT spreadsheets are formatted into four columns that coincide with the acronym: Strengths, Weaknesses, Opportunities, and Threats. It's often recommended to use this tool before committing to any company action, and it can be used to help with everyday decisions as well. For instance, if you're trying to decide on a career path, you can write out your strengths and weaknesses. These are internal factors within your control. Then, list what doors are currently open for you (opportunities) and which are closed (threats). Those are external factors.

There are two ways to evaluate the results: matching and turning. Matching is when you find a competitive advantage by connecting the answers in the strengths column to the answers in the opportunities column. Turning is when you try to turn the negative answers into positives. For instance, if under weaknesses, you wrote, "I suck at economics," consider whether you can turn that negative result into a positive by taking courses and enhancing your skills. Once you turn your negatives into positives, you can go back and find even more competitive advantages.

Another great way to enhance skills is through internships and job shadowing. Consider those in your list of opportunities! There's no shame in unpaid internships and job shadowing. They're both incredibly valuable and are great ways to know what you're actually getting yourself into with the career you're considering. It's great to test the waters to gain experience and see if it's a good fit. If you can, try to do multiple shadows and internships! It's good to see the differences and similarities within different companies, especially if one company has a super toxic atmosphere (they might not all be that bad!) or one feels very recreational (some other companies may be more strict!). And if you're still questioning if it's for you, speak to mentors!

Mentors are always a great asset to have. Conversations with mentors can provide clarity and propel decision-making. The best mentors are role models who exemplify the kind of boss you want to be (literally and metaphorically). They're people you respect that you can trust to guide you along your career path when you need help deciding which direction to take. Whenever your inner voice is shouting, "WTF do I do next?" or "I don't know if that job is really me!" ask questions! It's never silly or naive to ask questions, but being afraid to do so is silly. You can learn so much by sitting down and listening to the steps your mentors took to get to where they are today.

Now that you know the tools you need to take the next steps toward your goals and see your opportunities more clearly, it's important to stress that you must jump on those opportunities as soon as possible! Stop procrastinating. Procrastinating is POISON for career building. It's essential to keep your ass moving (I see you hitting those squats, get it girl ;)). If you're the type to hold yourself back by procrastinating, setting deadlines is a great way to whoop that rump into gear. Setting deadlines forces action and prevents endless deliberation. Write down your immediate goals and come up with realistic dates in which you would like to accomplish them - AND STICK TO THOSE DEADLINES. If you need to work on your résumé, treat it like homework. Give yourself a due date! Setting dates for your goals will keep you on track. Reward yourself when you make your deadlines, so you have an incentive! Do whatever you can to GET THE WORK DONE!

If you are anything like me and even after trying these tips, you STILL find yourself procrastinating, fear not. Drastic times call for drastic measures, and I have just the one! Coined the "Nothing Alternative" by fellow procrastinator and novelist Raymond Chandler, the idea behind it is simple. You don't HAVE to do your work, but you can't do anything else. And I mean NOTHING else. No social media doom scrolling, no checking emails, no getting up to grab a snack (you're not hungry, you're just bored), just nothing. Lay the dreaded work out in front of you and either do it or stare into the abyss. The idea behind it is that you will be so overcome with boredom that, eventually, you will CHOOSE to do your work.

In the harsh words of Arnold Schwarzenegger in his book *Be Useful*, "Rest is for babies, and relaxation is for retired people" (yes, we all read that in our inner Arnold voices). I am all about rest and relaxation when it comes to mental health, but when it comes to career building, he is absolutely right.

1.5 ACTION OVER PERFECTION: A CASE FOR "GOOD ENOUGH"

Remember when I told you that the dream job is a myth? We're now going to get a bit more granular with that while I slap you in the face with this reality check: There are RARELY any jobs that check off ALL criteria for "the perfect job"! You have to take the good with the bad.

In the TV series *Apples Don't Fall*, Annette Benning's character Joy Delaney said, "There will always be reasons to leave. The question is, are there more reasons to stay?" She was saying this in the context of her daughter's relationship (which is solid relationship advice), but this question also applies to jobs. There will always be ups and downs with every job. There may even be days you want to quit, but if the pros outweigh the cons, the job is probably good enough to stay.

Don't turn down a job opportunity just because it isn't perfect. PERFECT DOES NOT EXIST (I know- ouch). However, "good enough" does exist, and sometimes you need to take the job that is just that: good enough. If you don't, your résumé will not be good enough to get you ahead, and your bank account might eventually not be good enough to pay your bills (Again, ouch! But someone needs to tell you this).

In terms of your résumé, it helps to make incremental progress so you can fill that bad boy up with your experience. Never feel inferior for making incremental progress. Realistically, you won't get where you want as soon as you would like, and that's okay! Sure, Billie Eilish now has TWO Oscars at 22, but the MF QUEEN Jamie Lee Curtis didn't win an Academy Award until she was 64! She was in about 50 movies before she reached that goal.

You're not going to reach the top of the success ladder overnight, but that doesn't mean you won't eventually get there by taking small steps. Don't quit just because you're frustrated with the length of the journey. You still get the medal when you finish the marathon, no matter how slow you crawl to the finish line.

There's a famous principle called the Pareto Principle, aka the 80/20 Rule. Vilfredo Federico Damaso Pareto, an Italian philosopher and economist, discovered it. One day, Pareto noticed that 20% of the pea pods in his garden produced 80% of the garden's growth. This led him to wonder if this is a typical distribution pattern. He studied further and found that 80% of Italy's population dwelled on 20% of Italy's land. He also found that 80% of production came from 20% of production. I'm sharing this with you for two reasons. (1) Knowing this principle can help you to see that you should prioritize options that deliver the most value. It can also help you to see that (2) Just because you're not getting results fast enough doesn't mean that giving 100% isn't working. If Pareto was correct, 20% of what you put forward will produce the best outcome, so don't get discouraged if you feel like you're at a standstill 80% of the time.

There are plenty of successful people who have thrived after settling for the "good-enough" path:

- Oprah Winfrey studied speech communications and performing arts in hopes of becoming a TV journalist. She landed a TV news anchor role but was fired several months later and "demoted" to a morning talk show. She settled for that "good-enough" job and ended up finding her voice as the billionaire Oprah Winfrey we know today.
- Julia Child was always more interested in sports than cooking and had several career reroutes before she went to cooking school. First, she was fired from her advertising position at a home furnishing company. She then tried to join the military but was told she was too tall, so she volunteered with the O.S.S. to develop shark repellent used for underwater missiles in World War II. It wasn't until she met her husband at work and followed him to Paris that she found her love for French food. It took 10 years of hard work and rejection before publishing her cookbook.

You see, settling for a job that's good-enough does not mean that you are giving up. It means that you are resilient and able to roll with the punches. Don't get discouraged if you play career roulette and land on an opportunity that doesn't check all of your resilient boxes because what you landed on might be the start of something great.

[2]
THE DIGITAL DILEMMA AND ITS DESIDERATUM

2.1 DIGITAL LITERACY: A NON-NEGOTIABLE SKILL

Most of you reading this book were probably born around the time Facebook was born, so you wouldn't remember how it started. It has changed a LOT since Mark Zuckerberg founded it in 2004, and so has its counterpart, Instagram.

Facebook used to be a place for students to connect with other students. For a while, they only shared photos, and little was known about the repercussions of posting, so most college students posted wasted pictures of themselves at frat parties (uploaded from digital cameras). Yes, your older cousin or aunt might have had photos of herself chugging beer bongs on Facebook! Hopefully, she deleted those...

Instagram was released six years later and was used mainly by artistic souls to share washed-out hipstamatic photos of rocks and water. It was a big deal at the time because nobody had seen digital photos with a vintage look.

It was all innocent friend-to-friend photo album exchanges, but then the statuses came (which were still personal). Your same relative might have regrettably posted something like "drunnnnkjsdf!? PIZZA". Again, hopefully, deleted.

As time went by, advertisers swooped in, and Instagram became the land of influencers, and Facebook became a bottomless pit of information and misinformation posted by boomers.

Social Media and digital technology are changing at a rapid exponential rate, and 92% of employers require digital skills, so the last thing you should do is ignore it (unless you plan on becoming a self-sufficient farmer. But even if you do that, I still think you should read this so you can learn how to make money posting that incredible lifestyle).

Once upon a time, social media connected only family and friends, but now it connects colleagues and brings in business. Because of that, there are now so many other facets of digital technology used in the workplace: video conferencing, e-commerce, digital marketing, artificial intelligence, and so much more. All of these tools increase productivity and connectivity, so keeping up and becoming a digital ninja is a sure way to ensure that you are an asset to employers. The more you know, the more employable you will be.

Taking a digital skills assessment is a great way to get a jump start on your digital education. There are plenty of online tests, including this one on the European Union website.

Once you know your weaknesses, you should enhance your

skills through e-learning. There are plenty of online courses (many of which are free) on platforms like SkillShare, Class Central, Open University, and even Stanford (yes, Stanford University generously offers some free online courses).

If you don't have time to take courses or find yourself in a panic attack because your boss just asked you to run a digital presentation over Zoom, you can always learn quickly by watching YouTube videos on your headphones in a bathroom stall (though I don't recommend that kind of procrastination).

I know you must be rolling your eyes because you obviously know that YouTube tutorials exist, but the point is that you NEED to make a point to continuously use tools like that to constantly continue your education. Even if you already consider yourself a wiz in your field, move on to another area in case your boss throws you a curveball one day! Just one 5-minute YouTube video per night could enhance your skills.

Learning should never stop when it comes to technology. The more you know, the more opportunities you'll have when you spin the wheel. Hey, if grandparents (who learned to type on typewriters) can keep up, then so can you. Seriously. Look at @baddiewinkle's account. She's 95 and is SLAYING on Instagram with 3.1 million followers. Goals.

2.2 SOCIAL MEDIA: THE DOUBLE-EDGED SWORD

When used leisurely, social media is addictive as hell, so deleting the apps altogether can feel like a spiritual cleanse. Have you ever tried to do that, though? I once tried it, and it felt incredibly freeing until clients and employers asked me to check out Instagram accounts or find the latest TikTok trends. Suddenly, I was in a desperate rush to re-download the apps, and immediately after finishing my tasks on Instagram, I found myself doom-scrolling and watching loads of reels.

The Digital Era is fucking complicated. We're told that spending too much time on social media is toxic, but we're also told that it's such an important tool. So what are we supposed to do?!

Keeping up your digital skills while learning to avoid unhealthy habits is crucial. You should use social media to help you, not hurt you.

There are several options for personal vs professional accounts:

- **Open**: transparent and authentic accounts. In other words, posting whatever the f*ck is on your mind for anyone to see with no concern for consequences.
- **Audience**: Separating your personal and private accounts, filtering what you post to each.
- **Content**: An account with an exceptionally curated professional persona (least authentic option).
- **Custom**: Manage both your audience and your content (create custom lists within your account and filter which posts go to which lists).

Which is right for you? Well, it depends on your career and how much you care about your professional brand. You might think that Audience sounds like the best option for you so you can be you on your private account and professional on your public account, but what if your co-workers become your friends? There are so many blurred lines, dammit!

Custom and content are recommended, but they must all be tailored to how you want to be perceived, which is what we'll get into in the next section.

2.3 ONLINE PRESENCE AND PERSONAL BRANDING 101

Now that we've stressed that there's no running away from social media let's dive a bit deeper into the world of personal branding.

I'm sure some of you think that sounds so corporate and phony and would rather eat a bowl of spoiled clams before selling yourself out like that. Honestly, I felt that way, too, until I was taught how to authentically brand myself in a way that would attract clientele but not disgust my current social media friends.

Freelance work is growing at a rate 3x as fast as the rest of the workforce, which means personal branding is a crucial tool to stand out from the competition.

You've got to confidently show off what you've got. I don't mean flash your tatas with a "free the nip" hashtag. I mean, show the world your skills. If you don't already know what your niche is, let's figure that out right now.

1. **Know your brand vision.** What do you want to be known as? Are you the compassionate philanthropist? The hilarious lawyer? The spiritual teacher? Combine your personality with your career to develop an authentic personal brand that is genuinely you.

2. **Know your brand mission.** What is your purpose? Do you want to empower fellow motivational speakers? Do you want to raise money for a non-profit? Know what the driving forces and goal outcomes of your brand are.
3. **Know your brand message.** What is the message you want to communicate to your audience? Are you trying to show them you are an original artist? Are you trying to teach empaths how to shield themselves from narcissism? Are you trying to prove to the world that anyone can be a crypto investor? Consider what advice you have that you want to be the beating heart of your content.
4. **Know your brand personality.** Try not to teeter-totter back and forth between the no-nonsense professional and the free-spirited wanderlust. You'll confuse the fuck out of your audience and lose them. Write down your strongest personality traits and choose how you want them to shine consistently through your content.
5. **Know your audience.** According to professional personal branding gurus, nobody likes someone who is desperately trying to be friends with everyone (Ouch... I feel seen). You need to figure out who would benefit the most from what you have to offer because not everyone is an ideal client. Once you've figured out who that is, dig further and research that group's demographic, desires, and challenges so you know who you are speaking to.
6. **Create an irresistible offer.** I don't mean that in the threatening Godfather sense ("I'll make you an offer

you can't refuse." I don't care how old/young you are... Those are classic quotes). I mean, create an original offer from which your niche audience can really benefit. And make sure it is something that they see only YOU can offer them. It should be a combination of (a) what you love to do, (b) what you do best, and (c) what your audience wants most.

7. **Explain what you do in 5 words or less.** This one is self-explanatory, and this chapter is getting way too long, so please just do it in the space below. You got this.

_____

_____

Now that you know your brand inside and out, get to work and put it out there. Enhance your social media, start a website, and create free content. So many free platforms are out there to help you launch all of this.

Personal websites are the best way to look professional and grow your brand. It's a one-stop shop where clients and employers can learn everything about you, see your work, and make appointments. You don't need to be a website designer to create an impressive website. Platforms like Squarespace, Weebly, Wix, GoDaddy, and Canva provide templates and tools to make it easy.

Make sure the homepage clearly communicates your identity

and offerings. Create a personal logo, choose an image that best represents your product, and ensure easy website navigation.

Include services offered, an "About Me" page, free content, contact information, and a call-to-action so visitors can easily request your services.

Free content is the least self-explanatory of those page nuggets, so let's go into a bit of detail there. By free content, I mean videos, podcast episodes, music, blogs, etc. There are so many free ways to create free content, and free content is the best way to show off your skills. Pumping out content is the best thing you can do for yourself. Not only does it allow your audience to see your capabilities, but it shows that you are proactive. I'd go into detail with each of these, but that's a book in itself.

You want to get a call-to-action out of your website, so offering an easy way for your audience to work with you is crucial. Use your website to allow clients to make appointments for free initial consultations, include a link to attend a webinar, and let your clients add themselves to your mailing list.

Make sure you add your website to all of your social media platforms and get a few professional headshots for all your pages and bios. You never know what kind of opportunity you'll land if you tastefully flaunt your talent and beautiful face.

2.4 CYBERSECURITY FOR BEGINNERS: SAFEGUARDING YOUR DIGITAL FOOTPRINT

Cybersecurity. It's the ick nobody wants to talk about, but everybody absolutely needs to address. Seriously. It's so damn easy to turn a blind eye, click accept on all terms of use, and allow every website to eat all the f*cking cookies it can devour. Just because you're in a rush doesn't mean being complacent is okay! If you have time to scroll and browse, you have time to be safe and use proper protection.

Right now (yes, NOW!), get your computer out. Open up all the browsers you use (Safari, Chrome, Internet Explorer, Firefox, etc...) and **switch to private mode!** It's unbelievable how few people know this, but you can browse all those applications privately. They each have their own form of private mode, all using the word "private" except for Chrome, which calls it *"incognito mode"*- just like the shady browsing option in Tinder. When you browse in this mode, your information is not saved, not even your history.

While you have your computer out, **change your default search engine to a private one** as well! You do not have to use Google! Yes, Google is now a MF verb, but that doesn't mean that it is the only reliable search engine, just like Ziploc isn't the only brand of resealable plastic bags. Plenty of high-quality search engines allow you to search anonymously, such as Startpage and DuckDuckGo (and there's nothing wrong with buying other brands of sandwich bags).

If you don't already have a VPN, it's time to start using one. **Download a VPN app** such as ExpressVPN or NordicVPN. These allow you to browse on a **v**irtual **p**rivate **n**etwork. And here's a bonus tip for your VPN connection: Use a less densely populated city as your home base. Large cities such as New York and Los Angeles are the default, and the connections are much slower due to high traffic.

Before you close that computer, there's just two more layers of extra protection:

(1) **Use quality antivirus software.** Most computers already have antivirus software, and that software is kept up to date to protect you from the latest hacking methods, so make sure to frequently update that sh*t.

(2) **Use strong passwords.** I know it's a running joke how websites require such intricate passwords, but they're actually watching out for you. It's actually suggested that you use 12 digits in your password (and dammit, don't use your phone number!). Have different passwords for different sites so hackers don't discover a one-size-fits-all password. Save your passwords in a little notebook instead of in your Apple notes. I know it's a major pain in the ass, but having your identity stolen is a much more painful pain in the ass.

While we're on the topic of identity, I have to stress that you need to **be careful what you post on social media** (I know. SIGH! You already got this lecture). This time, I mean in terms of your personal information that hackers can steal, which will give them all the answers to your security questions. For instance, on Facebook, don't share your hometown. And definitely try not to post your mother's maiden name or any of the other nonsense that websites ask for added security measures.

Alright, now that you are in a private network using a private search engine on a private browser, with strong passwords and an antivirus condom to protect you, it's time to move onto your cell phone. You need to use the same measures for your browsers on your phone. Also, **use a passcode for everything**. I know, it's annoying AF to type it in every time, but you can spare the extra three seconds to keep your shit safe. Just do it.

Finally, while browsing in general, be careful what you click!

THE DIGITAL DILEMMA AND ITS DESIDERATUM

There are so many phishing scams. Before clicking a link for a security break warning, make sure the message is coming from a legit source! There are so many scammers out there who will mimic your banks and subscriptions (like Amazon and Netflix) and send fake emails to ask you to click if you didn't try to purchase something. Search the source before you click anything.

2.5 FROM DIGITAL CONSUMER TO CREATOR: MAKING THE LEAP

Now you know how to create a brand and how to stay safe, so let's put that shit to work! It's time to become a content creator. Stop scrolling and trolling. It's a waste of time. It's a terrible habit, and it's bad for your health in so many ways. Just stop. It's time to be more productive online.

Creating content is one of the best ways to gain a clientele and stand out. Put your work out there! Let everyone see what you are capable of.

Remember when I mentioned you need to add free content to your website? Let's get to work on that! Blogs, podcasts, webinars, livestreams, video channels... There are so many options. Figure out which tool best suits your expertise and your voice, and get to work. Do you have tips for preparing taxes? Create reels and YouTube videos! Do you have loads of testimonials you'd like to share with the world? Talk it out on a podcast or write it out on a blog.

Not only are these great ways to showcase your expertise, but they are also ways to increase your cash flow! If you learn how to navigate all the available platforms, you can make cash simply by sharing your content. We'll get into all that money talk later. For now, let's just focus on launching your platform.

If you've completed all of your worksheets, you should have a pretty good sense of what content to create, so let's get you started. Below is a list of options for you to choose from. Start with whichever tool best communicates your message, and once you feel ready to take on another task, move on to another tool simultaneously.

It's much better to get really good at one of these options than to overwhelm yourself with too many projects. I can tell you from experience, the latter can quickly become a mess, and you could risk having loads of content pages with few followers and little content (that's what happens when you jump in without first having a wealth of knowledge from books like this one. You're welcome.).

Before you jump into any of these options, remind yourself what your brand is, who your audience is, and what your message and mission are. You need to know these in and out so that you have a FOCUS. Even the best platforms that feel like they are just rants have a throughline and understand their audience. Emma Chamberlain's *Anything Goes* is meant to seem like it's random, but she has topics that she knows resonate with her audience. Bill Burr's *Monday Morning Podcast* sounds like a grumpy middle-aged guy complaining about whatever peeved him that day, but again, he knows who he is speaking to, and his tone is consistent. Be consistent. Have purpose.

Back to your options:

- **Blogs:** If you're like me and your thoughts are much more clear when regurgitated in written form, blogging may be a great option for you. Several of the website-building platforms also offer templates for blogs. SquareSpace, Weebly, and Wix are examples. If you want to design a website and start a blog in one swoop, those are great options. If you only care about creating a free and easy-to-create blog, WordPress is your best bet. Before jumping in, know how you want to outline your blog. Once you know your focus and format, research popular search topics and create compelling headlines. Search Engine Optimization (SEO) is so important when it comes to creating successful content.
- **Video Channels:** Create a YouTube channel for your niche! If you can build an audience on YouTube, it can also bring in side hustle income (which we will cover in another chapter). TIP: Whenever you record for YouTube, center yourself in a way that you can easily change the aspect ratio for Instagram and TikTok reels (aspect ratio is a fancy pants editor term for the dimensions). That way, you can share clips on social media to bring in subscribers.
- **Podcasts:** Love to talk but hate to be on camera? Podcasts may be a great option for you. All you need is a laptop and a quality microphone. Do your research to figure out what works best for your office and budget. I highly recommend the Blue Yeti. It's easy to set up and

record quality sound. It also travels well since it's so sturdy.

These are only three of many options. Do what works best for you and stick to it. Your audience will only keep following you if you're consistently creating new content.

You'll also need to constantly promote your content. SELL, SELL, SELL. Instagram and Facebook Business offer easy and cheap advertising options. Take advantage of this and provide an easy call-to-action link in your ads.

[3]
BUDGET LIKE A BAD B*TCH

3.1 UNDERSTANDING YOUR MONEY MINDSET

Whether you like it or not, you are in a lifelong, committed, dependent relationship with money. Each of us has a different kind of relationship with money. Some have a loving, healthy relationship, while others have an unhealthy, neglectful relationship. Just like our romantic relationships, our relationship with money is influenced by early experiences.

Did you have to work hard for your money with chores and part-time jobs, or were people very generous to you? How did your parents speak about money? Was budgeting something your parents/guardians openly talked about? Was money always an issue, or was it just taken for granted? I'm not giving you another excuse to blame your problems on your parents, but how you were brought up and what you witnessed early in your life very much influences the foundation of your relationship with finance.

Just like any mindset learned at a young age, you have the power to reverse it as an adult. If you have an unhealthy mindset about money, you, and only you, can change that. Examples of healthy mindsets:

- "I have financial freedom but can also say no to purchases."
- "I give to those in need."
- "I am not in a financial competition with anyone."
- "I can and will reach my financial goals."

No matter your background or who you surround yourself with, nobody can change your mind about money but you. Your partner can lecture you as much as they want, but it's up to you to believe that you have the power to achieve your financial goals.

How exactly can you change your mindset? Well, you can only truly change if you understand where you're coming from, so let's take a moment for you to investigate the roots of your money mindset. Take out a journal or open a fresh document on your computer and answer these questions:

1. What is your current relationship with money?
2. What were you taught about money as a child?
3. How did your parents treat money?
4. What would you like to take away from your parents' relationship with money?
5. What would you do differently than your parents?

Once you understand where you're coming from and what you need to change, seeing your goals will be much easier.

Here are some other ways you can change your money mindset.

- Read books on financial psychology.
- Give money to those in need. (This will have an incredible impact on your life in multiple ways.)
- Dream of your retirement.
- Believe that success is possible.

It may be harder for you to believe that success is possible if your parents always struggled with money or if, the total opposite, you were always just handed money, and suddenly, that stopped. Money flow is never guaranteed, but hard work can turn financial hardship around.

Never get too comfortable with abundance. Sh*t happens in life that is unexpected, so you need to respect money and have a budget. However, having a scarcity mindset is also unhealthy. You need to stay positive. Budget your money, but don't live in constant fear. You must find a healthy balance and do your best to keep a safety net of money so you can afford to play the game of roulette again, even when life throws you curveballs.

3.2 THE ART OF BUDGETING WHEN YOU HATE NUMBERS

No matter who and where you are, even if you're happily living as a self-sufficient farmer, you need a budget and emergency funds. Nobody is absolved of those needs. Nobody.

Look at Schitts Creek! Yes, it's a fictional show, but the stakes are real. You can be filthy rich one day and live out of an old, dirty motel the next. Sh*t happens. Prepare for it.

Starting this week, I want you to begin implementing the 50-30-20 rule. It's a simple way to break down your spending by dividing your earnings into three categories: Needs, Wants, and Future.

- **50% of your income should be used for NEEDS**. That includes housing, bills, food, transportation, and healthcare.
- **30% should go towards WANTS.** Social life, spa treatments, extra clothes, vacations, etc. It's healthy to let yourself enjoy your income in moderation!
- **The final 20% is to invest in the future you**: savings, investments, paying off debt (your mandatory minimum debt payments are NEEDS! Use this 20% to pay more off your debt whenever possible).

The 50-30-20 rule isn't a strict commandment; it's a guideline that you can adjust to best suit your lifestyle. If your bills are significantly low compared to your income, you could afford to save more and/or spend a little more on wants. If you're drowning in debt and are barely keeping your head above water with the bills, you may need to sacrifice most of your "wants" so you have more to divvy between your bills and debt (I know, ugh).

The earlier you start budgeting, the better. I wish I wasn't so stubborn when I was younger and was given the advice I'm giving you. When I was only 23 years old, I was lucky enough to quadruple my income overnight via a fat promotion. One week, I was walking dogs after work just so I could afford food. The following week, I was making six figures. I got way too used to the abundance too quickly and spent a lot of my earnings on clothing and nights out with friends (I was 23 years old in Manhattan. It felt right at the time!). Five years later, when I finally grew up, I decided I wanted to move and change my career. Had I listened to my older colleagues, I'd have had a healthy safety net for my life transition, but instead, I was financially drowning since I had barely saved and had hefty student loan bills following me wherever I went.

Don't make the same mistake I made. Enjoy yourself, but KEEP A BUDGET! The 50-30-20 rule is a great guide for beginners, but there are also other tools you can use, such as budgeting apps and budgeting notebooks. Yes, actual notebooks with pens and paper! Sounds excessive and archaic, but seriously... It helps. Big time. If you write your goals in your handwriting, you are 42% more likely to accomplish them, and if you write down everything you spend, you are 98% more likely to say, "Holy sh*t! I've spent $2,548 on matcha almond lattes this year?!?!" (Yes, those drinks add up, homie. You could be going to Ibiza with that much money! Or paying off your debt so you can have the freedom to go to Ibiza anytime you want!)

There are plenty of budgeting apps to choose from to help organize all of your credit card accounts, bank accounts, loans, and bills (**Note: If you've been using Mint or were planning on using it, I have sad news. As of March 23, 2024, that app is no longer in service)

The following are excellent options approved by Forbes & the Wall Street Journal. They are in no particular order:

1. **NerdWallet:** Similar to the deceased Mint app. It's totally free and is very easy to use (hence great for budget virgins). Like the deceased Mint, it links all of your accounts and automatically categorizes expenses. It's great at its job but isn't as proactive as other apps.
2. **YNAB (a.k.a. You Need A Budget):** Follows a zero-based budget system. Rather than tracking past expenses, it helps you to plan for future expenses based on your income and goals.
3. **Good Budget:** Based on the envelope-budgeting system. It allocates your money into separate categories (or "envelopes") based on your budgeted portions (the way your grandmother used to organize her cut-out coupons).
4. **PocketGuard:** Like NerdWallet, this allows you to link all your bank accounts and keeps track of bills and spending. The only problem is that you have to pay for some of those features.
5. **Honeydue (for couples):** Allows for financial transparency for couples. Both parties' bank accounts and transactions can be seen in one app. Couples can also link bills and communicate about finances via the app (whether this is a good idea for you and your partner is an entirely different book).
6. **Empower Personal Dashboard:** Empower is great for keeping track of your net worth. Also great for detailed

analytics of cash flow and portfolios (I'm looking at you, investors).

Try a few of these and see what works best for you! There are so many tools out there to make budgeting more manageable, so why not take advantage.

3.3 SMART SAVING STRATEGIES FOR FUTURE FLEXIBILITY

Remember how I recommended that you start budgeting right away so your frivolous spending doesn't kick you in the ass later in life? The same goes for savings. It is so damn important to have savings. Wiser adults always told me to save my money. To an extent, I listened. I'd put cute amounts in my savings account each week, but since I didn't budget well, I often had to transfer that money back to checking. Rookie move, y'all! Budgeting and savings are dependent on one another, so if you neglect one, you'll eventually f*ck over the other one too. Budget and save! Say it again. Budget and save! Nobody wants to hear it, but if you have an emergency and suddenly can't work... or if you feel like you're on the verge of a nervous breakdown and want to switch careers or leave town, you need to have a decent amount of savings.

What's a "decent amount"? **It's recommended that you keep a consistent 3-6 months of expenses in a high-yield savings account.** That's 3-6 months of rent, utilities, transportation, food, loan payments, everything. When you're starting out in the workforce, and your savings account is 3 digits or less, 3-6 months of savings can sound very daunting when you're struggling to get by. Everyone has to start somewhere. Just breathe and know that any little bit you can add each month will eventually add up. $10/week untouched is $520/year before interest, which is a great start!

Consider what you can sacrifice in order to save. Do you really need a new pair of Sambas? Must you buy that $6 coffee beverage whenever you meet your friends or seek a change of scenery for your remote work situation? No! Your true friends will understand if you don't want to spend money you don't have, and there are free options for workspaces (like libraries and hotel lobbies).

There are always costs that can be cut. How many streaming services do you have? Consider canceling the services you use the least. You can always resubscribe or use a friend's account if there's a new show you're dying to binge!

I'm not saying that you shouldn't treat yourself to the small joys in life. I'm just saying... don't overdo it, especially if you have no savings or have big financial goals.

Enough of the lecturing. I know how nauseating and eye-roll-inducing the "Save your money" talk can be. It's just better to understand it now rather than learn the hard way later in life after you gamble it all away (literally or metaphorically).

Now, back to the more tangible advice. I mentioned high-yield savings earlier, and I know some of you secretly thought, "WTF is that?" It's basically a savings account that accrues more interest, so you end up with more money than you put into it! Sounds great, right? So many people neglect that option and just use the same bank as their checking account because it's just easier to have a one-stop shop. Those savings accounts are great for cute things like vacations, but for emergencies and life changes, you want the higher APY (annual percentage yield).

There are plenty of quality online **high-yield savings accounts** to choose from:

1. **American Express Savings** (who knew they have more to offer than the platinum lounge and travel perks)
2. **Barclays** (like the basketball and concert arena in Brooklyn)
3. **Sofi** (like the insane football stadium and concert venue in LA)
4. **Synchrony** (aww)
5. **Bask Bank** (save now, bask later)

Pick one and get it in! (not like that, you perv.)

3.4 DEMYSTIFYING STUDENT LOANS AND DEBT

Fuuuu*k student loans! Oof. Sorry. I just had to get that out before we talk it out. Actually, I suggest you do the same. Quick. Grab a pillow (right now!) and scream into it. Feel a little bit better? Good.

Student loans are like STDs in many ways. Nobody likes to talk about them, and you've probably met more people suffering from them than you think. However, there's no way to ignore them.

Sometimes, it feels like you'll be paying off student loans for life, but you know what? F*CK that. It's time to make those loans your b*tch.

If you're reading this and you haven't even applied for college yet, you can tell from my trauma-dumping rage that it might be wise for you to avoid student loans whenever possible. Apply to as many grants and scholarships as possible, and ask your parents to be transparent about those co-signed loans they've applied for so you don't get a nasty surprise after your college graduation. If you know ahead of time that the loan bills are coming, you'll be able to plan for them, so try to be as informed as possible about your college finances.

If you've already graduated from college and have begun paying those bills, it's still important that you are constantly in the know about your options.

First, you need to know the difference between private loans and federal loans.

Federal loans are provided by the government. Whenever you hear Biden discuss loan forgiveness, he is referring to these loans and only these loans.

Private loans are provided by banks, credit unions, and other financial institutions. The interest is often higher, and there are less loan forgiveness plans for these. Try to avoid them whenever possible.

Here's a few tips for navigating the shitty world of student loans:

1. Before you pay another dime, **see if you qualify for any loan forgiveness programs**. If you work for a non-profit or the government, work as a teacher or healthcare professional, or have a permanent disability, you may qualify for loan forgiveness. Check studentaid.gov/manage-loans/forgiveness-cancellation to find out.
2. **Apply for income-driven payment plans.** Federal loans have the SAVE program that allows for smaller payments for low-income households, and most

private loan companies will also adjust to your income. **If your income decreases, notify your lenders immediately** so they can lower your minimum payments and potentially give you a forbearance.

3. **Pay more than the minimum whenever possible.** Most minimum payments include just a drop more than the interest, so by paying the minimum, you will end up paying a lot more money than the loan's original amount. Whenever you can, pay more to keep that interest down and speed up the repayment process (unless the loan has zero interest).

4. **Prioritize the highest-interest loans.** When you can afford to pay more than the minimum monthly payment, put more money towards the loans with the highest interest rates. You want to pay those off first.

5. **If your payment is going to be late, CALL!** For instance, if you know that you will be unable to pay an upcoming bill, call customer service to inquire about options. Most customer service representatives are happy to hear that you are being proactive about your financial situation, and some will be able to change your due date, adjust your payments, or waive the late fee. Chatting to a human representative when you are in need never hurts.

If you are in credit card debt, the same rules apply (except for rule 1, and substitute the word loan for credit card). Always prioritize paying off the cards with the highest interest rate, and always notify the companies of income decreases and potential late payments so they can help.

If you are paying off multiple credit cards, **debt consolidation may be a great option for you.** There are plenty of programs, such as Lending Tree and National Debt Relief, that will give you **fixed-rate loans** so you can pay off credit card companies and make payments to a loan company with less interest. You could also transfer your credit card balances onto a **0% interest credit card** and pay that off.

Fixed-rate loans and 0% interest-rate credit cards can allow you to pay off your debt within 5 years. Sounds like a sexy option, right? But before you dive straight into this deep commitment, you need to be financially stable and obtain a high credit score. Otherwise, you likely won't get approved since it's vital you make every payment and avoid further credit card charges.

Debt is the biggest buzzkill, and so is talking about it. I'm emotionally drained after that! But I did promise I would be real with you.

If you take anything away from that huge stinky trauma dump, it should be that you need to avoid sinking into debt whenever possible, and if you are already in debt, do whatever you can to keep the interest low- and don't EVER be afraid to seek help.

3.5 INVESTING IN YOURSELF: SKILLS OVER STOCKS

Remember when I mentioned that 20% of your income should be reserved for "future you"? That doesn't just mean paying off your debt and saving your money. It also means literally investing in yourself!

No, this is not an excuse to spend money on self-care. Sorry, but that is a want. By investing in yourself, I mean spending time and money on education that will make you a more valuable employee.

Some options include staying up to date on the latest trends in your current field, taking courses on digital literacy, enhancing your personal branding, or learning a new skill set that's more in demand.

I've already stressed the importance of digital literacy and personal branding in the last chapter, so let's talk about those in-demand skills.

I know, I know. I just spent a whole f*cking section venting about student loans, and now I'm telling you to keep educating yourself. Just hear me out. You don't need to pay 5-6 digit prices to extend your education. There are plenty of online courses and tutorials for all these skills. There's even PAID education opportunities.

Seriously! Some employers will give you taxable income towards an education. There are also plenty of grants available, including Pell Grants, that cover the cost of most community college tuition. More information on paid opportunities can be found on Investopedia. Check it out!

Now, let's get back to discussing what to study. If you have the time and patience to tackle new skills or are considering an eventual career change, knowing what skillsets employers are searching for may be helpful. According to Forbes, the following are the most in-demand skills for 2024:

1. **Generative AI:** Whether we like it or not, AI is improving at an exponential rate. So where does that

leave us? Well, us humble humans are needed to decide which opportunities are best for this technology. We're also needed to address the ethical concerns of AI and propose boundaries so we don't live the plot of Terminator (a classic film that revolves around a war between humans and AI- Cheesy. Entertaining. Frightening.).

2. **Sustainability Skills:** On the opposite spectrum, most companies are looking for green solutions that will make a minimal impact on the environment, so learning about sustainability and green energy is both a marketable and ethical skill.

3. **Project Management:** Luckily, AI doesn't yet have the power to ensure Karen from accounting sets her differences aside with Tom from marketing so they can complete their tasks, so it's still up to us to put on our boss pants and find problem-solving solutions.

4. **Communication Skills:** Similar to project management, it's important to have communication skills as a general business skill. Being the liaison between departments and suggesting communication techniques for improved workflow is crucial.

5. **Clinical Healthcare Skills:** Um, we all know doctors, nurses, etc., are always in demand. No need to explain.

6. **Data Skills:** AI tools and computer technology are useless if the data collected can't be properly translated into accurate and useful information. That's where data scientists come in.

7. **Interpersonal Networking:** Building relationships with the right people who will help you achieve your goals is an essential quality. It not only helps you to achieve your personal career goals, but it can also help your employers if you're able to suggest people from your network who can get a job done. I know, networking is such a stuffy gag-inducing term for making connections, but it is extremely useful. Just do the world a favor and try to be authentic rather than manipulative in your techniques.

8. **Cloud Computing Skills:** With the increase of remote work and the need for shared access to files, knowing how to migrate businesses onto the cloud is a very desirable skill. (And while we're on the topic of cloud and easy access to files- get your nudes off your cloud! Now!)

9. **Machine Learning:** Despite the fact that there are now AutoMLs, Human MLs are still in demand to implement AI technology.

10. **Cybersecurity Skills:** Hacking and security breaches are becoming severely more frequent, so there's a dire need for cybersecurity skills to protect company and customer data (I repeat- delete your nudes!).

This list is merely to inform you of the predicted employment trends, so don't get discouraged if none of those are a good match for you. Just because these are predicted to be the most marketable skills doesn't mean they are the ONLY marketable skills.

Figure out what skills would best suit your personality and career, and keep learning. Knowledge is sexy, and the more you learn, the more opportunities you'll have when you spin the wheel.

[4]
THE ENTREPRENEURIAL SPIRIT UNLEASHED

4.1 THE SIDE HUSTLE STARTER PACK

With the skyrocketing costs of living and increased encouragement for self-care and passion projects comes the rise of the side hustle. Side hustles are great ways to feel fulfilled when your day job just doesn't get you off. It's also a way to (hopefully) earn extra cash.

There's been a major uptick in the usage of that term in the past 10 years, and thanks to digital marketing, it's becoming easier to turn side hustles into real profit. Soap-making and panty crocheting can now be more than just Sunday hobbies if, and only if, you do your homework and set up your business with intention.

Let's say you've been making bucket hats out of recycled leather for funsies, and suddenly, people on the street start asking you where you got your hats. You tell them that you make them yourself, and BOOM, you get the idea to turn your passion into a business.

You may be tempted to get started right away and post online that you're taking orders, but it would be wise to do your research first and make sure you're fully prepared. Otherwise, you'll have the embarrassment of back orders, unsuccessful branding, and (gulp) negative profits.

Below are some tips courtesy of The Muse:

#1 RESEARCH- Always research the market and the competition! Do people want leather bucket hats? How much could you sell them for? What would it cost to make one?

#2 ONLINE BRANDING- Let's rewind to personal branding tips! Know your audience, vision, personality, mission, and message. Once you have that narrowed down, create a logo and start promoting it on social media!

#3 TEST IT OUT- Start small! The last thing you want is to take more orders than you can handle or lose money on this new venture. Make just a few hats, keep track of the cost and time it takes to make them, and see if you can successfully sell them.

#4 CREATE A PLAN- Stay organized! Write down your goals and create a business plan. What are your short-term and long-term agendas? If you're successful, how would that look? Would you sell at makers markets? Would you like to sell to boutiques? How will you produce more hats to keep up with increasing demands?

#5 FINANCES- You need to be real about your finances. Plan ahead. Don't just wing it. How will you fund this side hustle? With your own savings? With your credit card? Crowdfunds? Think this through. If you choose a credit card, make sure you can realistically pay it off on time. If you borrow from friends or do a crowdfund, make sure that you are able to hold up your end of the agreement, whether that's payback with interest or prize incentives- stay organized and follow through!

#6 LONG TERM- Know your long-term goals. Don't be afraid to think big! How do you plan to keep your customers or expand your market? Do you plan on selling to stores? Would you begin making more leather products or hats from various fabrics to fit all seasons?

#7 ASK FOR HELP- Never be afraid to ask for help! If you have questions, ask a colleague who successfully launched a side hustle business (sh*t, even if they failed- ask them what happened so you don't make the same mistakes!) And if you feel like you're in over your head and need assistance, don't be afraid to expand and partner with others! You might feel like the side hustle is your baby, but it can be an even more rewarding experience if you share the passion with others.

Once you're ready to put your side hustle into action, you need to figure out your time management. "How the f*ck do I do this on top of a full-time job, family/social obligations, gym, and BS errands?" you ask. By keeping a strict schedule! Sounds overwhelming and militant, but it's not as bad as it sounds. Promise. You can start small by carving out just 45 minutes a day, a few days a week, that you dedicate to pushing your side hustle. Once you feel like you need to devote more time, increase those time blocks! Get up earlier if that helps.

Writing out your planned schedule for the day will increase your chances of following it, so write it out in a journal or planner and follow through! If you're afraid that your family/lover/friend/dog will distract you, shut yourself in a room, turn off your phone, or simply communicate that you'll be unavailable for that small time frame. If you don't put in the work, you'll end up with an Instagram account for a business you have no time for.

4.2 BOOTSTRAP YOUR BUSINESS: LOW-COST STARTUP STRATEGIES

Bootstrap business? WTF is a bootstrap business? If you're starting a business on your own without investors or any significant resources, you, my friend, are "bootstrapping." It sounds like a criminal term, right? Don't worry, it's not. It just means that you are building your company from the ground up on your own, which is f*cking awesome.

The idea behind bootstrapping a business is to leverage what few resources you have.

Social media plays a key role in expanding a business when you don't have a budget for marketing and advertising. Build your brand and post shareable content as often as you can. Post content that encourages the audience to engage and try to team up with influencers and brand advocates.

High-quality content such as blogs, infographics, videos, and ebooks will also help you gain recognition and attract clients.

Email marketing is another key tool. Start a list of email addresses of potential clientele or of friends/family/colleagues that would likely share the information. Make your emails personal so they encourage engagement and don't feel like spam. People are more likely to follow the face of a business than a brand (Elon Musk has significantly more followers than all of his companies combined). MailChimp is a great, easy-to-use platform for email marketing.

User-Generated Content is a great way to gain trust in your brand once a few clients have used your product or service! Even if you have yet to make any money, offer your product/service for free to a friend with a large following in exchange for a post! (In case you haven't heard the term UGC, it's a techie business term for testimonial reels and product endorsements).

Save money whenever possible. Use your home as your office. Keep your overhead as low as possible. Don't gamble all of your money away! Keep playing the game until you win big.

4.3 FROM PASSION PROJECT TO PROFIT: THE HOW-TO

Side hustles aren't always passion projects, and passion projects aren't always side hustles. A side hustle might just be a hobby that you've turned into additional income. It might not even be a hobby. It might just be a second job because, dammit, you need more income! A passion project is something you pour your heart into and deeply care about. I truly hope that you, darling, are lucky enough to have a side or main hustle that keeps your fire burning. And if you have yet to reach that point in life and have something you know you are passionate about, I encourage you to chase that. Carve time out in the day just like I recommended you do to start a side hustle.

Whether it's making a documentary, starting a fundraiser, or writing a book on how to navigate endless career choices (heh), don't settle for your autopilot routine if there's something that you genuinely care about.

Yes, you need to pay the bills, and sometimes that means you'll be too exhausted to think about another project after work, but you can use the procrastination methods we discussed for just small amounts of time throughout the week. Do that, and I guarantee eventually, you'll get so sucked into your passion project that you'll lose track of time (goals).

Once you get the creative wheels turning on your passion project, it'll be wise to take a day to do some research on how to monetize it. What we don't want is for you to get so wrapped up in a project that you're racking up purchases on your credit card and depending on the universe to show you a way to get it paid off.

I'm not implying that you should neglect your spirituality. Keep harnessing that, but please be aware that sometimes you won't be given a magical sign because it's up to you to do your own homework.

Sit down with a spreadsheet and list the steps it will take to complete your project and how much those steps will cost. Include the time that it'll take as well. If you can't afford it, would you feel comfortable crowdfunding via platforms like Kickstarter? If you charge it to a credit card, can you assure that you'll be able to pay it off in a timely manner? [WARNING: Credit card debt can be even worse than student loan debt if not paid off right away. The interest is WAY higher, and credit card companies are much less forgiving of late and missed payments.]

If you crowdfund, be sure to include incentives and follow through with them. Keep a list of your donors that you'll have handy even after you've completed your crowdfund. If you can't afford to give your donors incentives right away, be sure to do it as soon as you can. Don't neglect your supporters! Send them updates and frequent thank yous.

Once you've figured out how to finance your project and are chugging along again, make sure you eventually take a day to figure out how to profit from your passion project. The best-case scenario is that you thought about this in congruence with the budget, but maybe you were just content that you could afford to finish the project, which was good enough for you. That's totally cool, but why not consider the option of making money if it's a possibility?

For instance, if you're producing online sketches, research how you can increase views and which platforms will pay you for those views. If you're writing music, copyright it and research how to profit from it. Could you sell to an ad agency? Could you benefit from YouTube views? Could you make it a TikTok hit or win a song-writing contest? Do your homework and figure out a home for your passion project that will fill your heart and your wallet (I know. Cheesy AF. But your passion project is your baby, so be happy with the choice you make).

If you are starting a media channel or podcast, **Patreon** may be an excellent option for making money. With Patreon, you could offer donors and paid subscribers content that can't be found on your social media pages or any other free sites.

There are endless options for whatever your passion project may be. Do your homework and figure out what's best for you, and most importantly, don't be afraid to put it out there for everyone to see! Use the personal branding and social media tactics we discussed to get all eyes on you.

4.4 NAVIGATING FAILURES AND SETBACKS AS A YOUNG ENTREPRENEUR

We discussed the fear of failure in Chapter 1. Now, it's time to discuss what to do when you actually fail because it's likely going to happen at some point.

What?! You thought I was going to sugarcoat it for you? Hell no.

I'm here to be real with you and tell you that, yes, you're going to get knocked down once in a while! It's not gonna be pretty when you face-plant on the lonely Rock Bottom Island, but you (and only you!) have the power to gracefully get yourself back together.

Life would be boring AF if you didn't fail once in a while. There'd be no lessons to be learned if everything was always perfect. The highs just wouldn't feel as rewarding if you didn't have to climb to get there.

Sh*t happens! You could be feeling a dopamine high one day- enjoying your fictitious dream job, feeling like you can finally balance and afford your work life, friend life, self-care, love life, family life- the happy ending you dreamed of! Then BAM, you get hit with the shitshow truck. Your new job decides you're not quite cut out for the company, your relationship crumbles, and you can't lean on social outings to lift you up because you can't f*cking afford them anymore. Sh*t, you can't even afford your bills! (I'm cursing a lot. I know. I'm just trying to get in the mindset of rock bottom here.)

Life is going to be a rollercoaster at times. I blame Disney movies for making me believe there's such a thing as blissful, eternal happy endings. Have you ever noticed that we never see what happens after the Disney princesses get married? Not sus at all... And did you know that the original Grimm's fairy tales that the movies were based on were incredibly morbid? Spoiler Alert: In the original version of Little Mermaid, Ariel had to kill the prince to get her voice back and then turned into seafoam for 300 years! Now that b*tch really had to be patient and resilient.

Alright, that got a bit off-topic, but you get my point now. It will be a rocky road, but whether you overcome it is all up to how you deal with it. Your failures are the perfect opportunity to learn lessons. If you were hired for a job and got fired, take a look at what went wrong. Did you prepare yourself for the job before you started, or did you just take your employment for granted? Maybe the job wasn't ever the right fit, and it's a blessing in disguise that you were let go!

And what about that failed side hustle? So you ended up with a f*ckload of debt and only 8 Instagram followers... Maybe there's a way to rebrand! Maybe you needed to do a bit more research before you jumped in. Take a step back and evaluate. Just be sure not to make any rash decisions while you're feeling emotional about it. Stop and breathe, even if it's for a few minutes. Once you've calmed yourself, you can make moves again.

I know it's insanely hard to take this advice when you're lying in bed feeling like you failed and there's not enough Xanax and trash TV to heal your broken soul, but know that during those sh*tty moments, you're not at a dead end. You're just taking a detour.

Know how to pick yourself up in situations like these. Sometimes, when you're feeling like you can't face the world, leaving the house for some exercise and fresh air is the best way to clear your head. Force yourself. Know that walking to the door and stepping outside will be the hardest part. Maybe go to your favorite isolated spot if that's your thing! Or talk to a friend.

Having a solid support group in these situations is extremely helpful. Never be afraid to talk it out. If you have a friend, mentor, family member, or therapist who is a great listener, give that person a call or a visit.

Most importantly, look ahead! Don't dwell on what happened, and don't let it define you. Keep moving forward. Einstein was denied a job as a professor (can you believe that?!), and Dan & Eugene Levy pitched their show for a year and were turned down by every U.S. network before Schitt's Creek was finally bought by the Canadian Broadcasting Company (CBC). Tits up!

4.5 THE GIG ECONOMY: MAKING IT WORK FOR YOU

When you have the choice between commuting to a 9-5 job every day until you retire or picking and choosing freelance jobs to suit your schedule, freelance can seem pretty glam, but there are definitely pros and cons.

PROS:

- Making your own schedule (to an extent)
- The ability to pick and choose clients
- Potential to travel and work remotely

CONS:

- unstable income

- lack of long-term benefits
- Lack of routine

Choosing to work as an independent contractor can seem very appealing when you consider that you can pick and choose your work to revolve around your vacations, but it's important to know what you're getting into.

Some weeks, you'll work through weekends because work is pouring in, and some weeks, you'll feel guilty for binging yet another murder mystery series because you're not sure when your next paycheck is coming.

Unless you're in a union, you'll rarely have guaranteed rates, and you'll often need to pay for benefits like health insurance.

I'm not trying to scare you away from gig work. I'm just telling you all of this so you know what to expect if you choose that lifestyle.

Freelance work can be very rewarding once you're established because you'll be able to pick and choose where and when you work. You'll be able to choose whether you want the job with great pay or the job that gives you the most fulfillment (and if you're lucky, you'll choose between multiple jobs that offer both!). It's all very exciting, but you should know that it will take time to get established.

Luckily, there are now multiple apps for freelancers. Upwork, Freelancer, and Fiverr are some of the more commonly used sites. Employers are even using LinkedIn to post short-term contract jobs.

When you set up an account on a freelance site, it's paramount that you **create a quality profile page.** Use the tips from Chapter 2 to figure out how you want to brand yourself! Your profile should include a professional photo, an enticing bio, links to your website and portfolio, and, most importantly, great referrals.

Once you have a quality page, it's time to **get some reviews!** Don't shy away from taking the $5-$20 jobs when starting out. Yes, there are jobs on those sites that pay $5-$20 TOTAL. That's because clients on those sites are not all business owners. They're also individuals who are working on their passion projects and may not be able to afford much help to get it done. Take a few of those low-paying jobs and give them 200%. Not only will you get great reviews on your page, but you'll help out a fellow go-getter.

Before accepting a contract for any job, be sure that you have all of your questions answered. You don't want to accept a job and find out later that it's more work or less money than anticipated. **It's essential that you and your clients are transparent with one another. Ask about deadlines** before you accept the job. Make sure that you can finish it by the date needed (Be honest with yourself!). **Keep an open communication about your workflow**, too. Ask your clients how much they want to be involved. Some clients are very hands-on and like to collaborate, while others just want you to get the job done and would rather not be bothered. Once you feel confident you can get the job done with the client, press that confirm button and get to work!

Once you've racked up a slew of 5-star reviews, you should get work more easily, and you can slowly start to request higher-paying gigs. Warning: this process can take a while! It could be a few years until you're at the point where you're turning down work. Just keep at it and keep working part-time or full-time when you're starting out.

I'm telling you to keep your other jobs initially because, unlike traditional jobs, the income is never guaranteed to keep flowing each week. Even when you're an established freelancer, there will be instability. You might have 6 jobs one week and then have a 3-week drought. The saying "When it rains, it pours" really applies to the gig economy. It's a CONSTANT game of roulette, so how do you plan financially? Hopefully, when you start out, you have a cushion of money in the bank and savings, but regardless, you should cut your expenses when you start working as a freelancer. Keep a very low overhead. Remember the 50-30-20 rule? See if that works with your cash flow, and if you notice that you need to adjust the percentages, switch the numbers around. Maybe you'll need to do 80-10-10 at first because you just need to make ends meet. Whatever you do, ensure at least 10% is going towards debt (if you have any) and savings.

You can absolutely live the freelance life if that's what you want. Just make sure you're mentally prepared for the lifestyle changes.

[5]
MARKETABLE SKILLS BEYOND THE DEGREE

5.1 DIGITAL MARKETING: WHAT EVERYONE SHOULD KNOW

In case I didn't stress it enough in previous chapters, let me beat you over the head with this again- You must embrace the digital era! There are two polar sides of the spectrum that you want to avoid:

1. Gluttonous Consumers: those who scroll feeds for hours
2. The Consciously Ignorant: those who are too cool or too old school to embrace the digital era.

I've been guilty of both at different times in my life. For a while, I was a gluttonous consumer. Then, I was convinced that the digital era was toxic, so I deleted all the apps for a while (a bit dramatic, I know).

The challenging goal is to avoid the toxic and embrace the potential. Rather than becoming addicted to the consumption, think of social media and digital marketing as an insanely helpful tool to help you get what you need. Make it your b*tch, not vice versa.

If you keep up with technology, you will always be more employable. We've already covered social media and personal branding. Now, it's time to explore current and future marketing trends in more depth.

SEO (Search Engine Optimization) is here to stay. What's changing is where it's being integrated. It was initially used mainly for headlines of blog posts, news articles, and websites, but due to the increased use of TikTok and Instagram as search engines amongst Gen Z, keywords and metadata (the components of SEO) are being used more frequently in social media posts in order to increase discoverability. This also means there's been an increase in SEO integration within photo and video captions, especially for influencer posts.

Influencers are also here to stay. Digital marketers are using influencers to build trust in their brands since people tend to follow people over businesses. This trend has led to the growth of niche influencers, which means it's getting easier for companies to find the niche audience they need to sell their product. Selling a special cream to get rid of toe fungus? There's probably a guy or gal somewhere on the interwebs that's famous for being vulnerable about his/her most intimate foot problems! Selling a particular deodorant for hairier pits? There's probably someone out there flaunting a lush armpit mane! There's someone out there for everybody, er... company.

Macro-influencers (those with 100K-1M followers) and mega-influencers (over 1M followers) used to hold all the power, but due to the increase of niche markets and target audiences, **nano-influencers** (1k-100k followers) are rising in power. Use this knowledge to help out your company, or hell, get out there and start your own niche influencing account! Make more money, honey!

AI Chatbots are a relatively new trend compared to the rest of the digital market, but they are becoming exponentially more advanced and more popular. Companies are using them as a tool to produce documents more swiftly. Some are even using them to write entire ebooks. Mark Zuckerberg's company Meta (which includes Facebook, Instagram, and WhatsApp) uses AI in beta. Sounds so sci-fi, right? FFS. "Meta has AI in beta." Makes my head explode. I'm sure some of you are wondering what that means, too, and no- beta is not a sorority chapter, nor is it an inferior male personality. Beta AI are the bots you chat with in the corner of your screen. Again, this could be a whole book on its own, but the moral of the story is that it's good for you to know the latest AI trends and familiarize yourself with how to use them efficiently.

Youtube Shorts & Meta Reels are other tools you must learn to use efficiently. Meta reels are the vertical videos you scroll on Instagram and Facebook (similar to TikTok videos), and YouTube Shorts are basically their version of that. YouTube continues to lead as both an entertainment source and search engine for young browsers (especially teens and kids), so companies are taking advantage and using Youtube Shorts as a short-form video marketing tool.

The digital marketing world is ever-changing. That's why it's important to keep yourself informed and to practice using the latest digital marketing tools. Take online courses, attend webinars, follow experts, and exercise what you've learned. Practice creating quality reels and using AI even if you f*cking hate it. Your parents/grandparents grew up with typewriters and rotary phones. Imagine if they applied to jobs while refusing to use the internet or smartphones. If they went from flip phones and dial-up internet and are now out there spinning the wheel, you can too!

5.2 CODING FOR THE NON-TECHIE: WHY IT MATTERS

There's no doubt that coding is an in-demand skill, and guess what? That demand is still rising. If you do a LinkedIn job search for software engineering, the number of job openings is always in the 4-5 digit range (I just tested it, and there are currently 16,000 software engineer jobs on LinkedIn alone).

If you're not into tech, coding can seem very intimidating. It can also seem nauseatingly dull compared to more creative or hands-on jobs. I had a friend who took a web design course in college, thinking she'd be designing graphics and picking fonts (cute and fun!), and she was sadly disappointed when she realized she'd just be copy and pasting bits that look like this:

>>> type(-46)

<class 'int'>

Not cute OR fun.

It's not for everyone, but it's something everyone should consider learning. Why learn coding if you don't plan on becoming a software engineer? First, there's the obvious answer: it will make you more employable! Even if your job doesn't require coding, you are statistically more likely to get a job offer or promotion. Companies know that it's a skill that's needed more each year, so they know that it's beneficial to have employees who can do it if needed.

Coding also helps you to analyze and solve problems. When you code, it has to be correct, and if it isn't, you need to break down the problem and find a solution. It sounds silly, but practicing code can help you to learn how to problem solve better in daily life. Coding in a work environment can also help you to learn how to be a team player since it is a task that involves a lot of cross-departmental collaboration.

There's also, of course, the practicality of having the skill. You'll understand the digital world better and can use your coding skills to build apps and websites. If you have just the bare minimal skills, you can even use it to enhance a website you built on a template platform like SquareSpace (most of those sites allow you to add code if the template isn't to your liking).

There are several types of code that are easier to learn for newbies.

- **Python:** This is widely used among coders and is well-liked for its versatility. It's also easier for beginners since its syntax (combos of letters, symbols, and numbers) uses English words.
- **JavaScript:** This code is great for beginners because its syntax is easy to learn. Coders can also see the code brought to life in real-time, which helps speed up the detection of flaws. Java is used on all modern browsers, meaning once the code is written, it can be used on any computer (not all code has that capability).

- **Scratch**: If the thought of coding still gags you and you need a gateway drug, Scratch can be your naughty friend who'll teach you the fundamentals of coding without actually making you code. How? Well, Scratch was designed for kids to learn the fundamentals of coding by using a block-based interface (aka easier tools) to build games, interactive stories, and animation (fun stuff!).
- **SQL (Structured Query Language):** This isn't a general-purpose language like the other codes used to build websites. Instead, it's used to retrieve data from databases. It's a general skill that's good to have or at least understand, and this code has a relatively easy syntax for beginners to learn.

These are just a few code options. There are plenty of others you can learn.

There are coding boot camps and online universities where you can learn code. These look great on your résumé! If you don't have time for a full bootcamp, you can find free video tutorials on YouTube instead. When learning on YouTube, I highly recommend working along with the video and repeating what you've learned after you've watched. Skills like coding take practice. It's tough to learn just by listening to a lesson.

Once you've begun your venture into the software engineering world, it's beneficial to have support from a community. Partaking in forums is a great place to go to ask for help.

5.3 PUBLIC SPEAKING AND PERSUASION IN THE DIGITAL AGE

I fainted in a speech class once. No lie. Could it be due to the fact that my hypoglycemic ass slept in and skipped breakfast? It's possible. But I'm sticking with my theory that my mortal dread of public speaking had a hand in it, and that's a hill I'm willing to die on! Luckily, I'm much more confident now. Between life experiences and various techniques I'll discuss in this chapter, I no longer get (as many) anxiety attacks.

The most helpful advice is to remember that the presentation is not about you. I know that might seem confusing. You might ask, "If I'm thinking more about the audience, won't I get more nervous?" No. If you think about public speaking as an act of kindness, it will trick your brain to get out of fight-or-flight mode. Again, the WTF light must be going off in your head... Let me explain.

The amygdala is the part of your brain that activates the fight-or-flight mode. The thought of having all eyes on you activates that part of the brain. It goes back to our prehistoric ancestors, who actually needed to fight or flee if eyes were on them because those eyes were often trying to eat them. Unfortunately for us, that prehistoric ancestral trauma still drives our brain (Great, more trauma for my therapist).

So, how do we keep our brain from associating the audience with predatory behavior? Instead of assuming we are being judged, we think about what we can say to the audience that they need to hear. Acts of kindness activate the vagus nerve, causing us to feel good and abort the fight-or-flight mentality. Hence, if we **speak as**

an act of kindness to the audience, we will likely calm down. Crazy, right? You'd think that would have the opposite effect! If you're feeling nervous before you speak, you're supposed to remind yourself that it's not about you. That part makes sense if you think about it... When you decide to sit through a speech, you usually do it to hear something that pertains to you or to learn something new. It's not like you sit through a seminar thinking- "I'm here to judge the f*ck out of this person's public speaking skills." Who does that?!

Eye contact is another helpful tactic that you'd think would make you lose your anxious mind on stage. It's recommended that you hold eye contact with a person for an entire thought or clause before moving on to the next person. That way, the audience members feel like you are talking to them all individually. How does that help you? Well, it's way easier to have a bunch of one-on-one conversations than to speak to a whole room, right? So when you practice this tactic, you yourself feel like it's a more intimate experience. The brain is f*cking fascinating.

To calm yourself right before you go on stage (in addition to reminding yourself it's not about you!), **breathe deeply** and slowly. It's advice that applies to so many problems. Just. F*ckin. Breathe. It helps. I promise.

There are plenty of ways to help yourself prepare for public speaking. **Practicing**, of course, helps. You want to know the material well enough to explain it conversationally. Again, think about how your presentation resonates with the audience instead of memorizing bullet points.

If you're nervous about how others hear your voice (even if you're not), you can **record yourself** and listen back. That way, you'll notice your nervous ticks and fillers. You'll be surprised by what you hear back. Ummmm. So, uh... Yeah.

If you have public speaking phobias or just want to get better, there are plenty of options to prepare yourself, even if you don't have an upcoming speech. **Improv** is actually a really fun way to help you stop judging yourself- and it's really fun! "Yes and" is the key principle of improv. It means that you listen and respond. That should be common sense, but so many people just wait to say something planned WHILE someone is speaking instead of truly listening and responding to what the person said. Not only is it rude to do that, but it makes the conversation less intimate and, hence, less fulfilling. Improv teaches you to not only do that but also stop judging yourself before you speak!

You can also take part in social clubs like **Toastmasters**, a non-profit group where members practice speeches in order to get over shyness.

Speaking to groups with confidence not only on stage but also in boardrooms, webinars, podcasts, and online presentations.

Persuasion techniques are incredibly beneficial as well. You want your listeners to believe you know what you are talking about. Speak with emotion. Use metaphors, analogies, humor, and personal anecdotes. These tips all date back to the Ancient Greeks, who were pretty damn good at spreading new ideas. It was Aristotle who came up with three components of persuasive rhetoric:

- Ethos- building trust by showing credibility (i.e., by sharing qualifications and personal anecdotes

    Example: "I've been picking up dog sh*t for 20 years."

- Pathos- connecting with the audience through emotion, compassion, and empathy.

Example: "The germaphobe in me cringes when I bend down to pick up the dog sh*t, but I do it anyway because I'm doing the community a service, and god-dammit, that feels good."

- Logos- appealing to the audience's logical reasoning by sharing facts and statistics.

Example: "Refusing to pick up dog sh*t is a public indecency which can lead to public shame and sometimes legal offenses. In Beziers, France, DNA tracking is used on feces of undisposed dog sh*t. Guilty dog owners are fined 32 euros."

Those examples were actually the words of Aristotle himself.

In addition to the persuasion techniques within the speech, you can use your body for further persuasion (not like that you perv!). Make eye contact as previously suggested. Maintain good posture. If the presentation venue permits it, use the entire stage (think TED talks!).

Public speaking skills have so many benefits, so get out there and start practicing!

5.4 THE POWER OF NETWORKING: BEYOND THE BUSINESS CARD

Networking is such a gag-inducing word. You just picture corporate mannequins in suits smiling with squinted eyes and shaking hands while discussing their recent triumphs on the golf course. Barf (no offense if you're into that).

That's what I thought for so long when anyone recommended I attend a networking event. I couldn't bear being around what I thought were just shallow conversations and fake smiles as a currency for exchanging business cards.

I was so wrong. Networking is insanely important and doesn't have to involve phony exchanges like that. In fact, it's better if you are authentic and find people you authentically connect with! Apparently (and luckily), I had been doing that all along in a less formal way. If I enjoyed speaking with someone and felt like I'd enjoy working with them in the future, I'd find a way to stay connected. It's been very beneficial and led to many referrals and employment opportunities. However, I wish I'd listened and been more intentional with it, so in this chapter, I'll share how you can do that.

Preparation is key. Whether you're going to a formal networking or social event, ensure you are prepared before you go.

- Have your **business cards**, mini flyers, and merch ready to be dispersed.
- Practice your **elevator pitch** so you're ready to promote your service, product, or employment skills.
- Always **lead with your achievements**. Sell yourself before you express your goals in order to gain credibility.
- **Learn about the people there:** attendees, speakers, and organizers. That way, you'll know who to prioritize meetings with and have some information about them ahead of time, which will help with conversation.

I know it probably feels icky to think about preparing like this for a casual social event, but it's good to be prepared for any networking occasion. Obviously, you won't want to come off as a networking brown noser or annoying opportunist at your cousin's baby gender reveal barbecue, but it's still good to be prepared for meeting interesting contacts and have your business cards stowed away with your essential keys, lip balm, and wallet.

Once you have your soft pitches ready, it's important to focus on how you present yourself on the day of the event:

- **Dress to impress!** "Dress for the job you want" is what they say, so if you're trying to get a job with a company, dress like the boss. That doesn't mean that if you're at a law school event, you should dress like Judge Judy, and if you're eager to become a politician, you should wear a Hilary Clinton pantsuit... Flaunt your own style tastefully and professionally.
- **Hold yourself with confidence.** Keep your chest up and head high.
- **Ask open-ended questions.** Don't ask yes or no questions or questions with simple answers. Asking more thought-provoking questions will allow a more memorable and engaging exchange.
- **Express gratitude.** Be enthusiastic and appreciate your conversations. This shows that you value the opinions of others and, therefore, builds mutual respect.
- **Initiate follow-ups.** If you're having a stimulating exchange, suggest continuing the conversation over coffee at another date before moving on to another

person. It's good to at least exchange contact information so you can follow up.

All of this networking is pointless if you don't follow up and follow through. Wait a few days and reach out to your new connections. Send an email. Set up a meeting. Connect on social media. Share your work.

Social media platforms are a great way to keep in touch (another reason why the personal branding tips in Chapter 2 are so essential!). Delete those photos of you taking body shots and shotgunning brews immediately, and use your platforms to maintain professional connections. Connect on Instagram. Connect on LinkedIn. Keep your accounts updated so your followers can see your latest accomplishments.

Staying on your network's feed in a positive way is a great way to keep in touch. Because of social media, I've been able to recommend many colleagues for jobs simply because I see what they're working on and where via THE FEED.

"Whaaat?? You mean my followers are actually following my life? Creepy."

Yes! So stop sharing s**t you don't want certain people to see, and start being your own hype man! You want to increase your chances of winning the game of roulette, not deplete your options!

5.5 CREATIVE PROBLEM-SOLVING AND INNOVATION

Being creative is a learned skill, not a genetic trait.

"But my mom says I got my creativity from my great Aunt Sheila?"

Your mom is wrong. You and your great Aunt Sheila have the same creative capabilities as your close-minded Uncle Billy, but unlike Uncle Billy, you and Aunt Sheila *allowed* yourselves to be creative.

There is no scientific evidence that creativity is inherited. However, extensive research suggests that creativity can be learned. Just like you can go from a couch potato to a marathon runner, if you make running a habit, you can transform a narrow mind into an open mind with practice.

If you haven't noticed yet, there's been several usual suspects that are recommended in each chapter: exercise, diet, meditation, therapy, community... Another repeat offender is... (drumroll)... journaling! **Brainstorming and journaling** are two great ways to allow yourself to freely express yourself. There's a great book for those yearning to be creative called "*The Artist's Way.*" It's incredibly popular for those looking to become creative and those who are creative but feel like they're having a block. It includes the author's personal anecdotes as well as worksheets, just like another great book I know (wink, wink). In that book, journaling is one of the first practices the author mentions. She recommends writing three pages every day when you wake up. I started that habit because of that book, and it's now a part of my morning routine. You'll be surprised how often you will stare at the page thinking you have nothing to say and suddenly find yourself on page 4 venting and brainstorming, realizing you need to put down your notebook and continue your day. It's incredibly cathartic and a great way to stop being so judgmental of your inner voice.

If journaling isn't your thing and you feel too hesitant to be expressive or philosophical, creative **problem-solving** is another great gateway drug to open your mind. Most people don't associate problem-solving with creativity; they associate it with intelligence. Therefore, if you're more of the pragmatic type, you may feel safer challenging yourself with a new task than journaling. Learning new hobbies, practicing new skill sets, and even playing challenging games are all great ways to enhance your brain.

Another way to enhance creativity is to **surround yourself with diverse and interesting people** to **create new experiences**. Sure, it's great to have a community, but if you're an American Mormon dentist who's into anime and you only hang out with other American Mormon dentists who are into anime, you can only learn so much from each other. In fact, when you spend most of your time with like-minded, similar people, there's a good chance that you spend a lot of time just validating what you already know. However, when you spend time discussing with people with different perspectives, you'll be able to make more creative interconnections and, hence, become more intelligent and creative. Likewise, if you visit new places and continually allow yourself to have new experiences, you'll be able to make even more creative interconnections.

Your narrow-minded Uncle Billy may think creativity is just for bleeding heart artists, but creativity is actually a learned skill that enhances ideation and the ability to problem solve, which means it's an extremely valuable skill for any career.

For those who prefer a more technical approach to creativity, several methods exist to enhance imagination. One is mind mapping- which is a sort of flow chart (No. A flow chart is not a chart to track your period). Mind mapping is a method used for brainstorming and breaking down a concept into smaller components. For example, let's say your concept is PERIODS, and you want to devise a clever marketing campaign for tampons. Your first branches might include the different meanings of the word period (punctuation, menstruation, past eras). Then you'd break each of those down into even smaller subcategories and keep repeating that step until you feel like you have enough ideas (or have just run out of room, whoops). You can use this flow chart to develop marketing ideas by making connections between the subcategories. For instance, under "past eras," you may have a branch that says "Jane Austen." You look across the chart and see that connected to menstruation is "mood swings," so you connect the two to talk about period drama (hm, I might use this one, so don't steal that from me). This tactic could be used for story ideas, slogans, jokes... really anything that requires creative connections.

Another corporate-friendly tool is SCAMPER, which is often used to generate new product ideas or improve existing ones. SCAMPER is an acronym (left brainers f'in love acronyms).

Substitute

Combine

Adapt

Modify

Put to another use

Eliminate

Reverse

Let's say you're working for the same tampon company, and they need a fresh product idea.

Substitute- Could you substitute the materials? Perhaps use a compostable wrapper?

Combine- Could you combine this product with another and make it multifunctional? A pad/tampon combo or a tampon that doubles as a s*x toy? (Hey, I'm thinking outside the box here.)

Adapt- Could the tampons adapt based on your flow and PH levels

Modify- What element can you change to make it better? Can you use stronger cotton so you only need one tampon per period? God, that'd be nice...

Put to another use- Could you use it for other industries? Perhaps make smaller tampons for first aid kits so 8-year-old boys don't have big-ass tampons up their noses?

Eliminate- Can you streamline production by eliminating an element? Perhaps get rid of the land-filling applicator?

Reverse- What if you reverse the use? (To be honest, I'm not sure how to do that with a tampon without disgusting y'all).

If you're looking at all of these options to enhance your creativity and still have an overwhelming mental block, I highly suggest taking an **improv** class. It not only enhances public speaking skills (as discussed earlier in this chapter), but it also helps hush the judgmental voice in your head when you're coming up with new ideas. Improv requires rapid responses, so it's extremely beneficial for all professions.

We've now armed you with enough exercises to enhance your creativity, so next time your uptight Uncle Billy tries to tell you he can't be creative, you can prove to him that he's full of s**t.

[6]
THE SELF-CARE CAREERIST

6.1 WORK-LIFE BALANCE: MYTHS, REALITIES, AND STRATEGIES

Work-life balance is a deceiving phrase. It suggests that work and life are separate entities. It suggests that when you are at work, which is roughly half of your adult life, you're in a black hole that's void of life, which is sad AF. If that's your "balance" mentality, you are already losing the work-life balance game. Sorry, but you need to hear this. The secret to a healthy, balanced life is not the amount of hours you work versus the hours you spend away from work. It's all about how you work and how you live. If you use your time at work to fulfill a sense of purpose, be mindful, build relationships, and serve others, you are living! And if you are doing all of those things outside of work, too, you are winning!

Balance is not about how many hours you spend clocked in versus how many hours you spend on self-care or with friends and family. It's about HOW you work and HOW you live. It's also about setting boundaries. It's about knowing not only when you need a goddamn break from work but knowing when to tell your friends and family you need to put your head down and get your work done so you can finish a task.

Balance is about integrating health into all aspects of your life. The whole stereotype of growing cellulite on your ass while you sneak fun-sized candy bars out of your secret drawer in your dank cubicle as the only slice of joy between clocking in and clocking out is SUCH a boomer concept. Those days are over. Thanks to millennials demanding more work-life integration, many companies are accommodating healthier lifestyles with additional perks and benefits like childcare, on-site gyms, remote work, and kitchens stocked with healthy food and beverages.

It's up to you to customize your approach to cater to your lifestyle and career goals. If you feel you need to prioritize taking care of loved ones and building a family, look for remote work or a company that respects those needs. If your goal is to be a badass boss, put in the work and make sure you don't succumb to the pressures to sacrifice your dreams.

The old work-life mentality implies that you should be a little less ambitious. That's really not the case, especially if your career gives you a sense of purpose. Some people who have the outdated work-life mentality may make you feel like you're wrong to put in extra hours to reach your goals. They might try to make you feel like it's unhealthy to be ambitious. It's up to you and only you to decide what balance works best for you. If you feel there's an imbalance, stop and evaluate. Is it the time distribution that's off, or is it your personal habits? Are you not carving enough time for family and friends, or are you just not mentally present enough when you are with your friends and family? Are you unhappy with your job because of the hours and benefits, or are you just not being mindful enough at your job? Are you forming unhealthy habits at work because it's an unhappy environment, or are there ways you can adjust your personal habits? (For f*cksake, get rid of the candy drawer!!)

If you feel overwhelmed or incapable of finding your personal solution to a balanced life, guess what, there's apps for it!

Headspace is a great app for mindfulness, meditation, and improved sleep. Those 3 ingredients are essential for a healthy life at home and at work.

There are also great apps to help you organize tasks at home and work. **Cozi** helps you keep track of family appointments, shopping, to-do lists, and meal planning, and **Trello** helps you manage projects, collaborate with team members, and prioritize tasks at work. You can also use **Calendly** to schedule meetings since it allows you to block out times that you're unavailable (Use this to set boundaries!).

For physical health, you can use apps like **MyFitnessPal** to set weight and nutrition goals and ensure that you're keeping a balanced diet and getting enough exercise.

Again, it's the usual suspects of mindfulness, meditation, exercise, diet, and community that really factor into your success at work and in life, so get to work and figure out what adjustments you need to make to maintain a healthy balance.

6.2 MENTAL HEALTH IN THE WORKPLACE: BREAKING THE TABOO

Another outdated concept is the taboo of mental illness. We no longer live in the 1950s when going to the "shrink" meant you were an outcast, and the slightest mention of mental illness might mean you'd be exiled to an institution. We, of course, now know that there is a wide spectrum of mental illness, most of which is treatable. We also know that with the right strategies and/or treatments, most with mental illness are perfectly capable of functioning.

What we still need to work on is the reduction of STIGMA, which is the feeling of disgrace and isolation. This starts within ourselves. If you have a behavioral illness, whether it's acute depression and anxiety or paranoid schizophrenia, it's important that you are kind to yourself and remind yourself that you are not an outcast or a burden and you are not a negative stereotype. Stop internalizing those negative thoughts. Be kind to yourself!

Openness is another way to eliminate stigma. If you have struggled with mental health, share your story. It'll help you and others who have had similar experiences feel less isolated and relieve the burden of internalizing your struggle.

Another way to decrease stigma is by watching your language! (I know thats rich coming from someone whos been cursing their way through this whole f*cking book, but thats different). It's fun to describe someone with a comical or wild personality as "crazy" or "looney," but when you use phrases like that to describe someone struggling with mental health, it just adds to the negativity associated with mental illness. I honestly can't remember the last time I heard anyone under 70 use the word "looney,"... but you get the point.

Equally important to eliminating stigma is your own self-awareness. It's so important to take care of your own mental health and to recognize signs that your mental health is impacting your work or your work is impacting your mental health.

Mondays often suck, and of course, Sunday nights can feel like a farewell to the weekend, but if you feel a sense of impending doom or overwhelming anxiety due to anticipation of Monday's work, that's a major red flag. Not everyone is lucky enough to have a job they look forward to, but if you're feeling intense symptoms regularly, that's a major red flag and means you need to evaluate the issue. What is stressing you out? Do you feel like you can't take breaks at work? Do you feel like work is heavily impacting your relationships outside of work? Do you feel disconnected from your coworkers? Do you feel like your growth is stunted at your job? Figure out if any of these issues can be resolved, and if they can't, it may be time to find a new job.

Accepting a job that sucks the life out of you as a part of life is both ironic and outdated. It's often normalized by early mentors, family, and even television and movies. Think about it. How many shows can you name that feature a dad (*cough* sexist) coming home from work irritated and treating his family like crap? Not only is it common, but it's often accompanied by laughter or labeled as heroic. Talk about validating toxicity... Don't be like the miserable TV dads that were normalized by older generations. Instead, find a fulfilling job with a healthy work environment and be present and kind to the people you engage with outside of work.

I'm not saying that you need to quit your job ASAP if you are unhappy. You NEED to evaluate first. See if there is anything you can change at work. Is it more of an internal problem than a matter of external factors? If so, what do you need to change within yourself? Can you make more of an effort to take breaks when needed? Can you talk to your boss or coworkers about any of your issues?

Seeking outside help can also be your answer. Talk to a therapist about what you need to change or see what mental health care your company provides. More and more employers are including behavioral health in their health care plans. Make sure you've looked into all potential outlets before you decide quitting is the answer (unless, of course, you already have a better badass job lined up).

6.3 THE BURNOUT GENERATION: SIGNS, SYMPTOMS, AND SOLUTIONS

Similar to the symptoms of anxiety and depression is BURNOUT. If you don't already know what burnout is, you can probably guess from the context that it's the result of physical and mental exhaustion. It's when your body and mind burn out from lack of rest and balance.

Extreme burnout can lead to mental and/or physical collapse, so it's essential to recognize and address the signs as early as possible (You can't win at career roulette if you're too burnt out to spin the goddamn wheel!!!).

Early signs include apathy, decreased productivity, neglecting needs, bad habits, and irritable behavior. More severe symptoms include depression, anxiety, sleep disruption, substance abuse, weakened immune system, extreme fatigue, and heart disease.

Many factors at work can lead to burnout. The first being the most obvious; long hours and heavy workloads. Lack of work-life balance, lack of control over your work, and working in help professions (like health-care) also play roles in burnout.

When you're early in your career, you may feel the need to push your body to its limits at your job. It's okay to be ambitious, of course. Just make sure to stay in tune with your body!

One thing I learned too late in my career is that it is okay to take breaks. Of course, not every job is so accommodating, but if you're on your feet and sitting is discouraged, take a short bathroom break to get a moment of rest when you feel like you need to recoup for a minute. If you're at a desk job, take periodic breaks to take your eyes off of screens and move your body, even if that means just moving your limbs at your desk. It may sound really silly right now, but when you're under pressure at your job, it's so easy to neglect what's going on with your body.

Even just changing your mindset can help. If there are factors at work that are stressing you out that you have no control over, accepting that you have no control can only help so much.

I know... easier said than done when you're working towards a deadline and Karen is really slowing down the team's progress, but just do your best to be aware of what you can and can't control and to accept it.

When evaluating how to prevent or recover from burnout, changing how YOU handle your workload is the first step. Evaluate if there's anything you can change. Are you taking on more than you can handle in order to impress your employers? Are you avoiding outsourcing work to other coworkers when that's the best option?

It's natural to want to be a stand-out employee and to prove your worth at work, especially when you're a new hire. Just be aware that if you bite off more than you can chew, it'll hurt you in the long run when you reach a point where you burnout.

In the early stages of my career, I'd volunteer for every task, and I never let my coworkers help me. Not only did that lead to physical exhaustion, but it made me look like I wasn't a team player. You must remember that you are not only there for your boss but also for your coworkers. If you need help with a task and your job allows you to do that task with the help of others, don't be stubborn. Take help if you need it. There's no shame in it.

Of course, burnout is not always due to your own mindset and actions. Sometimes, it's not within your control. Sometimes, the job itself is boring or overbearing, and staying alert is physically draining. Sometimes, there is a bullying coworker that you literally have nightmares about. Other times, it can be a lack of clarity of what's expected of you.

Dealing with burnout is very similar to dealing with mental health issues at work as it involves similar factors: work environment, work-life balance, health, and mindfulness.

Consider whether your work environment and task load can change. Are you able to discuss changes with your boss? Is there a coworker you can ask for advice? Maybe a mentor?

Also, consider if factors outside of work are triggering burnout. Are you getting proper sleep? Are you able to mentally escape from work when you clock out? Are you being mindful and present both at work and at home? Are you maintaining personal relationships and taking care of your health?

When you're healthy outside of work, chances are you'll feel healthier at work and vice versa. Stress at work can carry into your personal life, and personal issues can carry into your work. It sounds like such basic advice, but it's very often overlooked that you need to have health and balance in all aspects of your life in order to prevent burnout and stay healthy.

6.4 MINDFULNESS AND PRODUCTIVITY: A SYMBIOTIC RELATIONSHIP

So, I've mentioned being mindful in multiple chapters, but we have yet to really go over what that actually means.

Mindfulness is a term that's often misunderstood. It's often associated with yoga and meditation, so those who aren't into yoga and meditation might think "STFU" when told to incorporate mindfulness into their lives.

Yes, mindfulness does play a major role in yoga and meditation, but that's usually not what experts are referring to when they tell you that a healthy lifestyle involves living mindfully.

Mindfulness is all about being PRESENT. It means focusing on one task at a time and enjoying little moments. It is something that should be practiced both at work and at home, even for the simplest tasks.

I didn't understand mindfulness until a mentor gave me an example of washing the dishes mindfully. He said when you wash the dishes, instead of rushing the job and thinking about what you need to do next, put all you have into the task at hand. Wash dishes properly. Enjoy the moment. Turn on some music. Put some pride into the task so you feel great about those sparkling clean dishes when finished. It sounds lame, but seriously, that little suggestion really helped me to grasp what it means to be present.

When you do things mindfully, not only are you increasing the quality of your work, but you're taking care of your mental health. Those who are more mindful are generally much happier.

It's so f*cking hard to be mindful these days. Technology allows us to be accessible 24/7, so it's so damn hard to put down the phone and get into a workflow. Think about all the times you've stopped a task to look at your phone when you didn't even have any alerts. It's a terrible, unhealthy habit, but we've all done it.

Whether you are working, working out, enjoying a hobby, or chatting with a friend, try to **focus on what you are doing** rather than what is next. Fully engage with others. Listen and respond instead of letting your mind drift. Go for a run and turn off your notifications so you don't pause your workout to respond to texts. Do everything with a purpose.

Try to **avoid multitasking**. Yes, it's great to be able to juggle multiple tasks, but doing them simultaneously will absolutely yield a less desirable outcome. Complete one task at a time. If you get stuck and need to switch tasks for a moment or need a break, that's perfectly fine, but do your best to focus on one thing at a time.

It also helps to **watch your emotions** while at work. I say watch instead of regulate because being aware of your emotions is healthy. Bottling emotions can be super unhealthy, but feeling emotional while working can be distracting. That's why you should stop and acknowledge your feelings for a moment before continuing your work. For instance, if you're working on a proposal and your boss's attitude has been making you angry, recognize and accept the anger and continue your work. Know that your anger is distracting but will not disable you. Do not use your emotions as a reason to procrastinate, and do not let them fester.

When you take a short break, try not to multitask or mindlessly scroll. Instead, be mindful. Listen to classical music. Go for a short walk. Doodle. Let yourself daydream for a few minutes. I promise you'll feel much more fulfilled after a mindful break than you would after online shopping while doom-scrolling and stalking your ex (stop stalking your ex!).

Mindfulness is a proven way to reduce stress and ease depression. Directing your attention to the present moment while accepting and noting your emotions is both healthy and productive. Practice now- even while reading this book, dammit! Put that phone away.

6.5 SAYING NO: THE ULTIMATE CAREER AND LIFE SKILL

No! For a two-letter word, it's a pretty strong statement, and it's often considered to be negative and harsh. We're taught to be "yes men/women" and to be positive, but our time is limited, so it's good to pick and choose how we spend that time. When you say yes to something that does not serve you, you're actually slowing down your progress. Instead of doing everything and spending time with everyone, spend more time nurturing the relationships you care about most and choosing jobs and opportunities that align with your goals and interests.

Warren Buffett, one of the most successful investors of all time, has a famous listing technique he uses to narrow down priorities. I want you to do this right now. Grab a pen and paper.

1. **List 25 goals.** These could be broad goals or immediate goals.
2. **Circle 5** of those goals that are most important to you.
3. **Cross out the remaining 20** goals.

According to Mr. Buffett, you should base all of your decisions on whether or not it serves those top 5 goals, and you should avoid the remaining 20 goals at all costs! Bet you're rethinking those 5 goals now, but you're stuck with them... muahaha.

Let's look at an example. Let's say your top goals are "Pay off student loans," "Get a dog," "Get a real estate license," "Lose 20 pounds", and "Visit Jamaica." A respected colleague offers you a remote coding job that requires you to travel around the US. It pays slightly less than what you're currently earning, but the flexibility of working remotely combined with the excitement of travel sounds great. Plus, you enjoy coding and are sick of your current job. It's a tempting offer, but should you take it? Compare it to the 5 goals listed.

"Pay off student loans."- The new job pays less, so unless your cost of living will be less (unlikely if you're traveling), you'll likely not be able to pay off much more than the minimum monthly dues.

"Get a dog."- Since the job requires travel, this will make that difficult.

"Get a real estate license."- Would you have time to take the courses necessary? It depends on how flexible the remote hours are and whether or not you can do the classes remotely while traveling.

"Lose 20 pounds." Will you be able to maintain a healthy lifestyle with this job, or will it be too difficult to maintain a diet and workout routine if your routine is constantly changing? Only you know whether you have the self-discipline.

"Visit Jamaica"- It's less pay, so you likely won't be able to save as much for vacations.

Even though the job sounds enticing and you're afraid of letting your colleague down, this job most likely isn't a good fit for your goals.

It's okay to say no, and colleagues who are looking out for your best interest will respect you when you tell them that an offer doesn't work for your current path. Saying yes to everything is counterproductive since having too many tasks and opportunities can shield your focus, and most people will understand that. Of course, now and then, you will have a boss or colleague who has a more selfish or narcissistic view and will take it personally. In that case, I'm sorry you're dealing with that, and I hope you are dealing with that person in a healthy manner.

In order to say yes, you must be comfortable asserting yourself. **Assertion** is the ability to state a thought or belief with confidence. If you confidently say no and explain yourself with **clarity**, you're more likely to have your refusal received with respect.

You must also **be polite and show appropriate gratitude** in your offer rejection. It's good practice to begin your statement with a buffer of appreciation: "Thank you so much for thinking of me, but..." or "That's such a great offer, but..." Then **follow up with a concise explanation**: "...but I'm only taking clinical work at this time in my career."; "... but I'd prefer a job that doesn't require travel at this time since I have two toddlers."; "... but writing about furry fetishes doesn't serve my career as a political journalist."

Saying no can be really intimidating if you're not used to it. That's why it's great to practice. If you have time to plan, write down what you want to say. Practice it with a friend. Even if you don't have a major refusal coming up, practice saying no when social events aren't serving you. So many people say, "I can't afford to go to this bachelorette party in Vegas, but I HAVE to," or "I really should work on my thesis this weekend, but I HAVE to go to my 1-year-old niece's birthday party." If you can't afford the bachelorette party, a true friend will understand, and your 1-year-old niece will not remember if you miss her birthday. Will your friend pay your debt from the expensive trip, and will your family help you finish your thesis on time? Probably not! It's okay to say no when you need to. Start getting used to it, and know that when you say yes to everything, you aren't paying proper attention to the tasks and relationships that matter most to you.

[7]
ALTERNATIVE EDUCATION AND CAREER PATHS

7.1 VOCATIONAL TRAINING AND APPRENTICESHIPS: THE UNSUNG HEROES

Your parents and teachers might cyberbully me for saying this, but- COLLEGE IS NOT THE ONLY OPTION!

"You mean my education is a goddamn game of roulette too?!" Not quite. It's more like poker since you control your moves.

Older generations had less opportunities for college, and as a result, many boomers told their kids that they MUST go to college in order to succeed, even if that meant co-signing loans for six figures that they would never help you pay back.

I'm not saying that college is the wrong option. I'm just letting you know that you can and should explore all options for your career path before committing to an expensive degree. Do your research. Do not go to an expensive university with an undecided major just because you got in and feel pressured to do so (unless your family has a f*ckload of money to spend on college or you're confident that you'll figure it out within the first year. In either of those cases, you can take your core liberal arts classes while you decide).

College is not the only option for a quality education. Vocational training, aka trade schools, is an excellent option if you want to save money and enter the workforce sooner. Most trade schools only require a high school degree for admissions, allowing more time to decide what you want to study. Their programs are also shorter on average, with most running only one to two years.

Trade schools are great if you know exactly what you want to do or just want to start working ASAP because they have a very focused curriculum. The courses are all directly associated with your degree, so you don't have to waste time with liberal arts classes. I'm not saying that the additional courses required for a college education are useless. All education is beneficial, but if you want to enter the workforce sooner, you may want to choose vocational training over a college education.

The highest-paying vocations are radiation therapy, air traffic control, and dental hygiene. Other trades include plumbing, registered nursing, and computer programming (and, of course, there are many more options than that). Since these degrees and certificates are so specific and often can only be learned with the hands-on experience you receive in trade school, the jobs are usually in higher demand, and graduates can easily start work upon graduation.

There are, of course, pros and cons to trade schools. Yes, it is cheaper and quicker, but it does not allow the luxury of switching majors or transferring credits, so you need to know what you want before enrolling if you don't want to waste any time or money. If you take a few years off from college, you can usually continue your education down the road with few issues. You can also use your credits towards a degree at a different college. Trade schools, on the other hand, typically require you to stay on schedule, and since the trades are so specific, the classes are usually not relevant when you switch vocations.

7.2 ONLINE LEARNING PLATFORMS: TAILORING EDUCATION TO YOUR NEEDS

College and trade school are not your only options for an education. You can also partake in online courses. Woo!

Alright, it's not quite as exciting as living on a university campus or getting your hands dirty while on a vocational apprenticeship, but there are many benefits to an online education.

First, the **options are endless**. You can earn a degree or certificate, or you can just take individual classes. You can take courses through a single university or handpick from a buffet of online college and university courses on platforms like Coursera.

You can take courses to learn specific skill sets and also take courses on learning how to interview. You can take basic learning courses and courses on how your industry is changing.

Online classes are also much more **affordable**. Tuition is fairly low, and there's plenty of supplemental classes that are free. The schedule is also very **flexible**. Many courses don't involve live lectures, so you can learn at your own pace as long as you finish your coursework on time. This allows for a flexible schedule, which is useful if you have a full-time job and/or family obligations.

However, this means you HAVE to discipline yourself to keep up with your studies.

Degrees that usually require hands-on training or benefit from peer-to-peer interaction and class engagement are obviously better in person, but there are plenty of degrees that can easily be taught virtually. Education, engineering, marketing, and computer programming are just a few that can be 100% virtual.

One of the hardest parts about an online education is choosing from the endless possibilities. How the hell do you make your own schedule? How do you know how much time you'll need for each class?! It can be really overwhelming, but luckily, there are advisors at online universities just like brick-and-mortar universities, many of which are available to chat virtually (and I'm sure by the time this book is published, there will be AI advisors as well. Eek.).

Each class will likely take up at least 10 hours per week, or 15-20 if you're trying to make the dean's list. That means you have to be honest with yourself about the time you have available for classes. If you have a full-time job, 1-2 classes is likely your maximum. If you are able to be a full-time student, you may be able to take up to 5-6 classes, depending on the difficulty of each class.

Now, how the hell do you know WHICH classes to take if you can only take so many? There's usually a wide load of courses available, so choosing can be a challenge. While it may be tempting to sign up for "The Genius of Taylor Swift," it might be wiser to sign up for "Audio Engineering" and "Composition 101" instead. Choose the classes that will benefit your career the most. Remember the Warren Buffett goals list we practiced in Chapter 6? When you're signing up for a class, think about your 5 goals and whether the class will help you reach one of your goals.

ALTERNATIVE EDUCATION AND CAREER PATHS

Completing your courses will require a lot of discipline. You might be able to gain a virtual degree by doing the bare minimum, but you gotta absorb the material and practice it. Otherwise, what's the point? You are just wasting your time and money. This, of course, applies to any education, but since it's so incredibly easy to neglect your online education, I need to stress this the most to anyone who is considering online courses. Do the work and practice what you learn! It can bite you in the ass down the road if you get hired based on the certification on your resume and your employer finds out you can't actually do the work associated with that certification. You can watch YouTube videos on the company toilet for quick tutorials, but trust me, it will only get you so far.

There are loads of opportunities to earn a virtual education tailored to your needs and schedule. You just need to be able to discipline yourself.

7.3 THE CASE FOR GAP YEARS: PROS, CONS, AND POSSIBILITIES

We've discussed schooling options, but what if you still don't have a f*cking clue what you want to study? What if you're not ready to jump straight into another educational institution or a serious career? Maybe your parents were too controlling, and you need some space to figure out what you want. Maybe you're too overwhelmed by all of the decisions. Maybe you just want to save some money before you choose a school. If any of these scenarios apply to you, perhaps a gap year is in your cards.

WTF is a gap year? A gap year is a year of self-exploration through new experiences, typically for young adults. It often involves travel, volunteer work, or internships. Most gap years are spent abroad, but more and more young adults spend their gap years in their home countries and even hometowns.

As long as you are challenging yourself and genuinely using the year to do what you need to do to grow and decide what you want to do with your life, gap years can be very beneficial. How can you be expected to know what in this big wide world you want to do if you have yet to experience it? I'm not saying that it's impossible to know what you want before branching out of your comfort zone, but it is totally understandable if you're overwhelmed by the numerous possibilities and need to do some self-searching before you decide.

Gap years are a great way to take the space you need. Some people take a gap year after high school because they can't decide if college is for them. Some take a year off during college because they are overwhelmed or need to consider if they are on the right path. Some take a year after college because they aren't ready to take the leap from school life to career life. You can even take a gap year mid-career for many reasons.

Like any alternative life decision that veers from the traditional high school to college to career to marriage to baby to retirement scheme, gap years have a stigma (ugh). Your elders or peers might think you're being irresponsible or too sensitive. They might think you're too much of a drifter or dreamer. F*ck them. If you can afford a gap year and it's the right decision for you, forget the haters. They're honestly probably just jealous they never got to take a gap year for themselves.

Like everything else, there are benefits and there are drawbacks. If you're unsure what to do with your life, it might be a good option so you don't fall into a major or career cycle that isn't the right fit (As I keep repeating- why spend the money if you don't know what you want?).

Gap years are also a great way to get to know who you are by meeting new people and partaking in new experiences. When you're yearning to learn something new about yourself, stepping out of your comfort zone and learning from people different from you is one of the best things to do. It helps you to gain new perspectives on the world and yourself.

You don't need to take a gap year to have these experiences. Everyone should make it a habit to step out of their comfort zone and travel to new places. However, if you are lost and have the luxury of taking a gap year, it may be a great option.

I say luxury when describing a gap year because not everyone can afford the time and money. You might desperately need to earn income ASAP, or you might miss an opportunity for a scholarship or grant for college. Even if you work part-time in your gap year, it costs money to travel and to support yourself. Just make sure you have a budget and a plan before you embark on a journey.

Planning is essential. Even if you have a limitless budget and want to travel spontaneously, you must set some goals for yourself. Are you trying to figure out your vocation? Are you looking to have interesting conversations? Are you wanting to take part in cultural events? Know what your goals are. Of course, your journey may take you in a different direction, but you need to have purpose. Drinking and sleeping your way through the trip or, taking beautiful Instagram photos and staring at the likes and comments all day isn't going to get you very far. Have goals and create genuine experiences.

Once you decide to take a leap year, you need to block out any negative voices stemming from societal pressures and self-doubt. Yes, taking a year off isn't for everyone, but if you're making it happen, be proud of your decision. Don't feel inferior for falling a year behind in your studies. When you're young, you might feel pressured to follow a timeline, but that timeline isn't for everyone. You will turn thirty and have high school friends who who have divorced their high school sweethearts and are taking online courses for a new career. There is nothing wrong with delaying certain milestones and there is nothing wrong with making changes later in life. There's also nothing wrong with taking a gap year later in life!

As I've said, gap years are not for everyone. If you are rolling towards your goals and have a vision for your future, keep forging ahead! If you have somewhat of an idea of what you want to do and want to explore that at an educational institution of your choice, get that! If you want to become a nun or a monk, that's cool too! If you're lost and need some time to find your calling- take a gap year. Just make sure you plan it out so you don't end up stranded in a strange place. It may sound romantic, but that scenario doesn't always have a happy ending.

7.4 BREAKING INTO TECH WITHOUT A TECH DEGREE

We've explored formal education and informal breaks, but what about informal education? Not all careers require a formal education. There are ways to prove your worth without all of the time and money. The world of tech is a prime example of that.

It helps to have a degree in technical skills, but it isn't always necessary. Many coders and programmers are self-taught. We've spoken about e-learning in other chapters. This is where that really comes into play. You can learn so much on YouTube and other platforms, and plenty of programs can teach you to code. There's Codecademy, freeCodeCamp, and Code School, plus plenty of other bootcamps.

You can't just take one or two cutesy little classes and expect to get a coding job. Yes, the job is in high demand, but recruiters aren't THAT desperate. You will need to dedicate a lot of time to learning and practicing the craft. Then you'll need to prove that you know code, but how?

Building a website with a portfolio of your work is highly recommended. Since you are seeking a career in software development, developing your portfolio on a website would be wise. Your website should include screenshots and links to 4-10 of your best coding work. This should be YOUR OWN WORK, not copied work or work that was a team collaboration. Showing work that isn't solely your own is the biggest mistake you can make because it diminishes your credibility.

Your portfolio should be attractive and well-designed, demonstrating your attention to detail. It should also include an "About Me" section describing your personality, a few testimonials, credentials and experience, and contact information.

Having a portfolio is so essential because tech recruiters care so much more about the quality of your work than the quality of your formal education. If your portfolio is impressive enough, you will look attractive to recruiters even if you have yet to enroll in a single bootcamp.

I'm not suggesting that you don't need courses and bootcamps. There are several benefits to online programs besides the obvious benefit of enhancing your skill set. Many bootcamps and short-term coding programs promise to help you to find a job after your studies. Some even offer a refund if they fail to find you a job within a certain amount of time.

Like any other job hunt, you will need to persevere through loads of applications and interviews. Even though software development is in high demand, there is still a lot of competition out there, especially since it is a skill that can be learned without formal education. Don't give up just because you haven't found a job a month after creating a portfolio. Keep practicing and keep applying. Make job applications and coding practice a part of your daily routine until you get a job offer.

Like any other career, networking in the tech industry is extremely beneficial. It can help you gain new insight, learn about new opportunities, and make connections. You can do so by attending tech conferences and networking events, joining online tech forums, connecting via social media, or partaking in online coding challenges on platforms like HackerRank and TopCoder.

A tech career isn't for everybody, but if you're searching for a new career that is in demand and doesn't require an expensive education, tech could be of interest to you.

7.5 CRAFTING A CAREER IN THE CREATIVE INDUSTRIES

On the complete opposite end of the spectrum, from a practical and technical career in software development is a career in the arts. There are endless options for career paths in the arts, but the road to a successful career in the arts often involves rocky paths and requires a lot of perseverance. That does not mean it's impossible!

It is absolutely possible to turn your passion into a career! You just have to know HOW to turn your talent into a sustainable job.

The days of the starving artist are dead. It's another deceased stigma from older generations that considered artists to be penniless wanderers. Yes, there's a chance you may not make money right away and might also be into a nomad lifestyle, in which case you would literally be a penniless wanderer, but there are so many opportunities for creatives these days that can enable you to succeed.

The first step in pursuing a creative career is to CREATE! Nobody is going to hire you based on your skills unless they've seen that you can successfully create. If you're a filmmaker, start shooting. If you're an artist, start painting. If you're a musician, start recording music. If you're a writer, write. When you finish those projects, release them to the world. Of course, you will want to keep some material to sell, but it's more important that you first show the world what you are capable of creating. Social media, music and video streaming platforms, blogs, and personal websites make it fairly easy to make your work public.

There are plenty of ways to make money from your creative talents. Artists and artisans can make money through Etsy. Musicians and Filmmakers can make money through YouTube and gain clients through social media. Writers can start with small jobs on Medium and get work through freelance platforms. There are plenty of creative ways to sell your creative work.

It's very tough to find a full-time job as a creative. I'm not saying that there aren't any jobs available or that you shouldn't bother trying, but you should be prepared to work in an unsteady freelance gig economy if you want to make creative work your main hustle. Be prepared mentally and financially to have weeks and sometimes months with little cash flow. Keep your head high and your overhead low. It will be tempting to get used to the perks of higher income when you get your first big paycheck, but you MUST make sure you save money and keep your ear out for future projects when you are on a short-time gig. There will be times when you are not selling as much or aren't getting as many gigs. Know that it's usually a matter of timing. There's just coincidental periods where there's not much of a demand for your craft, and everybody in your craft is fighting for the same job or clientele due to the work drought.

The money flow is never guaranteed when you're a gig worker, but if you know you want to create a sustainable life in the creative industry, you can look into joining a union or guild. Joining a union is beneficial because you'll be protected by labor laws and wage minimums. You'll even get healthcare and 401K through some unions. See if a union or guild is within your expertise and look into the membership requirements. Carpenters, writers, and musicians all have unions. Even Uber and Lyft drivers will soon have a union.

For those looking to get into the film industry, the union or guild depends on which department and state you work in. For instance, if you're a sound mixer in New York, you would join Local 52, which covers "Studio Mechanics" on New York film and television sets. Unions not only guarantee wages and benefits, but they protect workers from being overworked or put in dangerous situations.

If you prefer to stick with the freelancing websites or have too many crafts to pick one union, you can use the Freelancers Union, a broader umbrella union for all freelancers. It doesn't have the same wage protections and benefits, but it offers resources for affordable health care and more.

Whether you want to be a union stagehand or an Etsy artist, know there are options for you. Just keep hustling and keep creating, and you'll find your path. Just know that it's a bit more of a gamble.

[8]
THE GLOBAL CAREER ADVENTURE

8.1 TEACHING ENGLISH ABROAD: MORE THAN A GAP YEAR

Since you get paid to teach English abroad, it's technically not a gap year, but it still has most of the benefits of a gap year. In fact, you'd probably gain more benefits. Not only would you be earning a salary, but you'd have a more cultural experience since you are teaching residents and living like a local. You also have the benefit of learning a new language and gaining international work experience, which looks great on your resume, especially if you plan to seek a different career abroad in the future.

Teaching English abroad is also great for your well-being because you are helping others. As we learned in Chapter 5, when discussing public speaking, doing good deeds for others activates the vagus nerve, which not only makes us feel good but also supports our immune system. Doing good deeds is also a great way to boost serotonin and dopamine levels, which decrease depression.

Since living abroad is usually much cheaper than living in the US, you will likely have enough money after living expenses and savings to travel on your days off. It's actually much more inexpensive to travel from country to country when living outside the US. For instance, if you teach in France, you can hop on an affordable train and travel to Spain, Germany, Switzerland, or Austria within a few hours. Likewise, if you teach in China, you can catch a cheap flight to the Philippines or Thailand for a beach vacation.

There are plenty of perks of teaching abroad, but that also means it is a privilege and has more requirements than a typical gap year. First of all, you need training. Just knowing English isn't enough to teach. You'll need what's called TEFL certification. Choose a legitimate TEFL program so you get proper training and are not ripped off. This certification will get you a job in most countries, but some also require you to have a bachelor's degree.

Know the requirements for the countries you aim to work in. In addition to educational requirements, visa requirements will also be required. Research a few of the countries you are interested in so you know which visa you'll need to apply for and what documents you'll need to collect. Some countries require a formal visa, even if you are just a tourist. Other countries even require vaccines, fees, and additional documents for entry. Make a list of countries you plan to apply to and list all the requirements. Since some visas take time, you may want to do all this before your TEFL certification. You'll also want to get a passport if you don't already have one, which can also take a few months.

As with any big move, you'll need to have a budget. If you're traveling with school loans, phone bills, and other monthly bills in addition to what you will be paying for your cost of living and travel expenses, factor that in. Even though food and rent are cheaper, you'll still need to budget. Have a cushion of money before you go in case you have any emergencies or unexpected expenses, and once you start earning overseas, keep saving, even if it's only 5-10% of each paycheck.

You will also want to research your host country's cultural norms and classroom etiquette. Culture shock and systemic differences are expected challenges of teaching abroad. For instance, in some Asian cultures, direct and public student correction is frowned upon because they believe in "saving face," so in those classrooms, you would want to correct a student privately (don't quote me on that, but please do your research!)

Discipline may be challenging, especially when controlling a new class in a new place with people who speak a language you don't necessarily speak. To add to this, many classrooms are understaffed, and many teachers show up feeling ill-prepared. Not all classes have a curriculum to follow, nor do they come equipped with class materials, so before you start teaching, have a broad idea of how you could run the class if you have no guidance or materials.

There will be endless challenges, but overcoming challenges and adapting to new cultures builds confidence and gifts you with a wealth of experience. Not only will experiences like this build your character, but they will look great to future employers, especially if you want an international career. Even if you are just taking a break from your routine career, the possibilities of great outcomes are endless. You could meet new friends, learn about yourself and other customs, gain experience, and expand your heart and mind. Even if it's a total disaster (it won't be; YOU GOT THIS!), you'll gain character, grow up, and have loads of stories to tell.

8.2 REMOTE WORK AND DIGITAL NOMADISM: IS IT FOR YOU?

Back in the good ol' pre-2020 days, when 'pandemic' was just a word in zombie movies, most employees were required to report to work at a given location for each shift, even if their job required zero to little human reaction. One benefit of the otherwise notorious pandemic was the expansion of remote work. Due to long agonizing periods of isolation, companies were required to think of creative ways to continue their businesses, and family and friends needed to find ways to have social gatherings via the World Wide Web. It only took a few weeks for Zoom to become a common noun and verb as it was widely used for professional meetings and social events when everyone was told to stay home (damn, I'm jealous of anybody who had stock in that company). Companies suddenly realized that they could spend less money on office space if more employees worked remotely, and employees realized they could make money working at home, which, for some, was a dream they had never thought would come true. Now that things are back to a new normal, many employees are demanding to work from home at least a few days a week, and wanderlusts around the world are searching for full-time remote work so they can become digital nomads.

Remote work doesn't always require a stable location, so traveling while working "from home" is becoming more acceptable and common. Many countries have taken this new trend as an opportunity to welcome foreigners who are working remotely, introducing digital nomad visas.

Getting a digital nomad visa can be tricky. You have to know the rules for the country you are applying to and ensure your employer will agree to allow you to work abroad. You also need to be confident that you can sustain that job or have a backup plan in case your digital nomad job ends. It requires a lot of homework, but if you are looking to travel abroad long-term or become an expat (the new word for immigrant), it is well worth researching. Not all countries have digital nomad visas. Do your homework to figure out where would be the best fit for you, and then go over any questions with the embassy and/or an immigration lawyer.

Budget hack: Most immigration law offices have free or cheap consultation fees ranging from $0 to $500. If you run out of time to ask all your questions at the first office, schedule another consultation at another one and ask your remaining questions.

Wherever you go, you will want to be sure that you have stable internet. That rustic open-air hut on the coast of Jamaica may look romantic and only cost $25/night, but check the reviews to see if other remote workers had reliable internet. You'll also want to be sure you are traveling distance to a town that can fulfill any mailing, tech, or office needs. Try to prepare as much as possible. Pack a direct connection ethernet cord in case you have a big meeting and a shitty wireless connection. Pack a portable ring light in case your AirBnB has really unflattering lighting. Pack an external hard drive, chargers, anything you can think of that will save you stress. You'll want to be proactive and plan ahead for potential work scenarios, especially if your remote work will be in a very remote location.

Finally, you want to make sure you can self-discipline while you are abroad. If you're a digital nomad, you most likely are a wanderlust and probably be very tempted to explore everything your new home has to offer. Of course, you should explore. That's all part of the experience. However, you have to regiment yourself so you get your work done or else you will lose that job and lose track of your career goals.

Try to create a schedule for yourself. If you have set hours for your job, that'll make it easier to stay on schedule, so perhaps schedule a day or two each week that you work in a local cafe or hotel lobby so you feel like you're experiencing the community while you work. If you have a freelance job where you create your own schedule, know what times you are the least distracted and take advantage. Be strict with yourself. If you are most efficient in the morning, roll out of bed and get right to work when you make your morning coffee, stay there and get that sh*t done. If your creative juices flow the most at night, give yourself a late afternoon curfew and do your work in the evening. If you get itchy feet at lunchtime, work in the morning and evening and allow yourself a few hours to run errands and roam around during business hours.

Know your limits! Know when you get tired, when you get distracted, and when you are most focused. Create a realistic schedule and stick to it. Being a digital nomad is a great opportunity, so treat it like the precious gift that it is and treat your job with respect. Remember, you are a boss ass b*tch, you are traveling abroad, you are working hard, YOU CAN DO IT ALL!

8.3 INTERNATIONAL INTERNSHIPS: A STEPPING STONE TO GLOBAL CAREERS

Teaching abroad and working remotely are great, but what if you could work your dream job abroad? Getting hired to work for an international company is tough when you don't yet have the right to work in that country, but you CAN get an internship in your field.

International internships are a great way to break into your industry globally or to travel while expanding your work experience. Not only would you gain work experience in your field, but you would also be able to see the difference between the workflow in the US and workflows abroad. Sites like IES Abroad offer internships that include room and board AND help you find work after your internship is complete. Most of these programs require a fee, but since they help with further employment, they are literally worth the money.

If you'd rather not pay $5,000-$15,000 for your summer internship, you can search for opportunities via traditional job-hunting sites like LinkedIn. Finding an internship would require you to hunt not only for your own internship but also for housing (gotta live somewhere). Hostels are great affordable options, and depending on which country you choose, you may even be able to find your own apartment for a very affordable rate. If you can find an internship and housing on your own (which I totally believe you can), I highly suggest asking if the company will pay for your airfare, especially if it's an unpaid gig (worst they can say is no). Otherwise, you will need to factor that into your budget as well.

Most international internships are, unfortunately, unpaid. Paid opportunities are very competitive and are usually offered first to individuals with the right to work in the country. If you are determined to get a paid internship, look into a short-term work visa or a student visa. Some countries allow students to work up to 20 hours per week. Figure out which countries interest you and look into their options. You may need to apply for a visa before you are able to get a job offer. Use the budget hack in the previous section and discuss your options with an immigration lawyer (or two or four).

8.4 VOLUNTEERING AS CAREER DEVELOPMENT: BUILDING SKILLS WHILE GIVING BACK

Volunteering as a part of your routine is proven to be a key component to a happy and fulfilling life. It builds a sense of community. It's an act of kindness. It's a healthy hobby... Someone could probably write a book about all the benefits of volunteer work, and I'm sure somebody has.

Doing good deeds feels great and is great for whoever you're helping. It's also great for your resume. It shows that you are active in your community and care about something other than your career. It shows you're a compassionate human being, god damn it.

I highly suggest that everyone volunteer more often. Even if you do it for the first time for some self-serving purpose, like you need it for an application, or it's for your boss's charity, or you just want to do an Instagram post to get your girlfriend back (cringe)... do it anyway. It's very likely that you will get more out of it than you went in for. If you don't already have a charity in mind or have an obligation to volunteer, consider what you care about the most or how you would like to give back. You could volunteer at a homeless shelter or after-school program. You could volunteer at a nursing home or an animal shelter. You can volunteer for an organization that fights to get rid of mental health stigma or for a charity raising money to cure an illness. Pick one. Do SOMETHING. Do not say you don't have the time. I guarantee that if you look at the screen time on your phone, there are a few hours you can spare each month to do something for others.

Not only does volunteering help your community, make you feel good, and make your resume look good, it helps to build valuable skills: leadership, teamwork, time management, adaptability, mentorship, communication. It might even inspire you to change your path.

There are endless opportunities to volunteer at home or abroad. You could join a renowned volunteer organization like the Peace Corps, Habitat for Humanity's Global Village, or GoEco. You can also look at opportunities organized by churches and schools or look up a specific organization, like a summer camp or conservation project in another country, and reach out personally.

Treasure Beach, Jamaica, is a town known for community tourism. Organizations like the Treasure Beach Women's Group welcome tourists as volunteers. In the summer, they run a volunteer health clinic that coincides with the children's summer camp, both of which accept volunteers.

There are many communities around the world that could use your help. You just need to do a bit of research and find out who to talk to.

Make it a point to volunteer locally or abroad as soon as possible. It's one of the best things you can do for yourself.

8.5 CULTURAL COMPETENCE IN THE GLOBAL JOB MARKET

There is a growing demand for employees to have what is called "cultural competence." Cultural competence goes beyond cultural tolerance, which merely involves tolerating people from different backgrounds. That's a really sh*tty bare minimum, right? Having cultural competence means you are able to actively listen to and communicate with those with other beliefs, customs, and behaviors. It means that you make an effort to understand people with different backgrounds and recognize and respect diversity.

In a global economy, this skill set is highly valuable as it's becoming increasingly important that employees are able to communicate effectively with diverse colleagues and clientele. With the US becoming more ethnically diverse and virtual interactions with foreigners becoming more frequent, cultural competence will only be more in demand with time. It's also imperative because we still, unfortunately, live in a world that is full of discrimination, so if we all make an effort to learn more about each other, we can help change that.

All the opportunities listed in this chapter can help increase your cultural competence: volunteer work, living abroad, and working abroad. Even just making an effort to learn about new cultures and meet new people whenever you travel can make a difference. You don't even need to travel to do that. In several previous chapters, we've discussed the perks of surrounding yourself with people from different backgrounds. If you only surround yourself with people who have similar backgrounds and interests as you, you are limiting what you can learn from other people. Make an effort to learn from people who are different from you.

When you travel and jump out of your comfort zone, you're more likely to be open to new experiences and chat with strangers, but you CAN do it every day if you try.

Active listening, empathy, and engagement are three key components that can help you have a constructive conversation (try to practice these in everyday conversations). Active listening means that you listen and respond. You don't listen for keywords while you daydream about what you want to say next and respond with some generic autopilot response that you think fits, like "Yeah," "Absolutely," "God, that's terrible," or "HAHA!" Listen and respond. Listen to each word. Empathize with that person. Try to feel what that person must be feeling. Then, engage in meaningful and thoughtful conversation. If you are discussing a topic that you disagree with, listen and respond. Do not come back with a combative response. Try to understand where that person might be coming from, even if you perceive their views to counter your views. Debates are perfectly healthy, especially when conducted calmly and diplomatically.

The key to understanding is not only experience but also education. In order to have cultural competence, it's important to stay as well-informed as possible. Keep up with current events and brush up on history. Conflict amongst different groups often has historic origins, so it's important to be well-informed so you can more easily empathize and engage.

Being open to understanding others and actively making an effort to do so doesn't just make you a better employee; it makes you a better person. Get out there. Meet new people. And keep learning.

[9]
PREPARING FOR TOMORROW'S JOB MARKET TODAY

9.1 EMERGING INDUSTRIES AND WHERE TO FIND THEM

By now, you should have an understanding of what skills are in high demand, but what about careers? Which industries are expected to grow? It's pretty clear that **IT, cybersecurity, and communication** are on the rise, and we'll always need **healthcare**, but what else? It can't all be IT and medicine.

The number one emerging industry is **hospitality, leisure, and event management**. The demand for event management is expected to rise more than 30% by 2031, and there's an increasing demand for social entertainment, so many more theme parks, museums, and tourist attractions are expected to open. That's great news for job seekers and for tourists.

Someone needs to build all of these new facilities, so **construction** is also on the rise with a focus on quality over quantity. Safe and environmentally friendly buildings that use renewable energy are the way of the future (can I get an amen?). Someone needs to sell the lots that are being constructed so **real estate** continues to thrive.

Despite the growing need for sustainability and a green economy, **mining and petrochemical** industries still play an integral role, as fuel is still needed for transportation and machinery.

It's no surprise that the **food and beverage** industry isn't going anywhere. People need to eat and drink, and consumers continue to demand new products that cater to their ever-changing taste buds and diets.

The new products need a way to get from the factory to your home, so **trucking and logistics** are also on the rise. Store shelves and shipping distribution centers need to stay stocked, so someone needs to plan and execute the transportation.

Consumers need a way to pay each other back for these emerging goods and services, and hardly anyone carries cash around anymore, so **banking and peer-to-peer lending** continue to grow. US banks are in need of new tech and marketing strategies to keep up with the demands of cashless transactions.

There has to be a way to learn about all of these industries, so of course, **education** is also on the rise. However, the focus has shifted from the brick-and-mortar establishments to options for private education and learn-from-home modules.

If any of these industries interest you, consider your skillset and how you can become a top candidate for one of these fields. If you're into business investments and want to get into trucking and logistics, consider what you can study to enhance that niche. If you're a food scientist and want to be ahead of the game, study the latest diet trends and health studies to create healthy, consumer-friendly products.

If you don't see your calling listed above, don't get discouraged. Within each of these industries is a plethora of job opportunities. Consider your skills and passions. If you're an artist, you're in luck because art galleries are a part of the growing leisure segment, and if you're an actor, live events are on the rise. There are so many jobs, probably even some you've never even heard of or considered. Go to LinkedIn now and search your interest under the job search bar. You should see some sort of pattern in the search results.

9.2 THE ROLE OF ARTIFICIAL INTELLIGENCE IN FUTURE CAREERS

Only ten years ago (maybe less), artificial intelligence was just considered a sci-fi movie plot. It was unfathomable that AI would replace our jobs and we'd have robodogs roaming the city streets and robots delivering food. We are living in the future.

AI is advancing at a rate faster than anticipated, and it's both fascinating and terrifying. Suddenly there are AI chatbots in the corner of websites (as if it wasn't already hard enough to chat with a human customer service rep- F*CK!) Artificial intelligence is taking over tasks from writing to graphic design and music composition, but if this keeps happening, where the f does that leave us?!

Luckily, there are still plenty of job markets on the rise, as we just discussed. However, the jobs available within each of those sectors will change. It is anticipated that the expanded use of AI will lead employers to have a higher demand for higher-paid jobs that require specific skills, such as STEM technology. This means it is vital to keep learning as there will be fewer clerical jobs since AI is able to take care of routine tasks like drafting paperwork.

Do not let this all discourage you from your current path. Keep chuggin' along as you have been. The secret is to be fluid. If there is a sudden shift in your industry, don't be afraid to get out of your comfort zone and switch directions. Keep learning to move with the times and keep enhancing your skill sets.

9.3 SUSTAINABILITY AND GREEN JOBS: THE NEXT BIG THING

While the sci-fi world of AI is enhancing, we still need sustainability to make the world a healthier place to live. In a way, this is the complete opposite side of the spectrum from AI since we are basically learning how to take a step back and use less energy. There's an ever-growing need for us to create ways to expand industries while respecting the land in a way that vibes with our indigenous ancestors. Self-sufficiency and minimalist living are becoming increasingly popular, but as a whole, society is way too advanced with consumption to be able to fully return to its roots. Therefore, we need to think of new ways to combine progress with sustainability.

This trend not only affects the job market directly related to environmental studies and green energy, but it also affects most industries. Sustainability has gone totally mainstream thanks to consumer demands. When choosing products, consumers often look beyond the product itself. They want to know that there's little waste involved and that the product was created locally and ethically. This means fewer emissions and fair labor practices (thank you, consumers!). It also means that more and more products are becoming recyclable and/or are made from recycled materials. This affects everything from the fashion industry to tech. Product designers and entrepreneurs should keep this in mind when creating new products. I've been slapping you across with this statement throughout multiple chapters- continue to educate yourself so you can keep up with the vastly changing trends in your industry!

Science is obviously a key component in the green energy movement, but what other jobs are directly associated with it and are anticipated to be in high demand? In addition to the obvious environmental engineers and conservation scientists, there are also skilled labor jobs. The two jobs predicted to be most needed are wind turbine technicians and solar photovoltaic installers. Both of those jobs require only an education from a community college or trade school.

Even if your job has very little to do with conservation efforts and sustainability, you can and should stay informed and do your part. Think minimalism when shopping. Buy only what you need and aim for less packaging to create less waste. If you're purging, only throw something in the garbage bin if you are absolutely sure that it can't be recycled or donated. Even stained clothing and socks that are too gross to donate can be recycled. Most communities have fabric recycling. Take the extra step and do a little research. Use less plastics. Use reusable containers and silverware for your packed lunches. Drive less and use your feet, bike, and public transportation more often. I could go on and on, but we're here to talk about your career, so I'll save the rest of the preaching for another book. Just make sure you stay informed on ways to conserve, not only so you can help the planet and impress employers but so you don't look like a jackass when your trash can at work is full of waste.

9.4 LIFELONG LEARNING: KEEPING SKILLS SHARP IN A FAST-PACED WORLD

When you graduate from college, trade school, high school, or wherever you were right before you entered the workforce, you shouldn't assume that the education chapter of your life is over. It's just not true. Okay, it's true for people who choose to just cap their knowledge and remain oblivious to change. However, if you want to excel in both your career and your life, you should keep learning. Learn new skills, learn about new trends, learn new hobbies. It not only makes you more employable, it makes you a more interesting person with more to talk about. Don't let your curiosity die. Keep educating yourself.

There are so many online platforms now that there is no excuse to have a one-off education. MOOC stands for massive open online courses. Thousands of them are available in a wide range of subjects, from computer science to business management to architecture. You can enhance your current skills or learn something new.

If taking an entire course sounds too overwhelming at this time in your life, you can also partake in a one-off workshop or sign up for a webinar. If you're busy, webinars are a great way to learn. Of course, it's better for you to be fully present and do one thing at a time, but if you're really pinched for time, throw on your Airpods (or, in my case, airpod, I instantly lost one of those little f*ckers) and listen while you do household chores.

Create your own personal learning plan. Refer to your list of 5 goals from the Warren Buffett School of Prioritizing and consider what courses could help you to reach those goals. If one of your goals is to sell your first book, take courses on writing and publishing. If one of your goals is to get a job in French, take French courses and become fluent. Figure out what lessons are in your best interest and create a timeline for yourself.

9.5 CREATING YOUR OWN OPPORTUNITIES: THE ULTIMATE CAREER HACK

With all of the emerging technologies, digital trends, remote work, artistic opportunities, and ever-changing job demands, there are so many options out there for different careers and lifestyles. There are SO many that we did not cover in this book (cut me some slack, that would be impossible). You might even have an idea of what you want to do that doesn't yet exist!

If you have an idea for a business or a job you've yet to hear about, you can be an entrepreneur or at least have an entrepreneurial mindset if you are positive and resilient enough. It takes a tremendous amount of bravery and endurance to make a new idea come to life. You must believe in yourself and keep believing in yourself and your vision even when others don't think it's possible.

Really, everyone should work on having the mindset of an entrepreneur. Even if you never plan on becoming a business executive, thinking outside the box and envisioning opportunities is highly valuable. It means that you are solution-oriented and perform well under pressure. It also means that you're likely better at collaboration since you have a curious mind and ask a lot of questions.

Your career will be a series of opportunities that you create for yourself. Yes, "the universe provides," but it's not like it's going to reveal a plan for you via an ad on your TV screen while you lounge on your couch watching rewatching Vanderpump Rules. You need to stay proactive so that opportunities open themselves up to you. Even if there isn't a specific opportunity, if you keep an open mind and view everything with a sense of potential and curiosity, you might see some gaps in the market that could be turned into a business venture started by YOU.

You know your skill sets and your potential. If you look at the current job market and see a way that you can apply your talents to consumer demands in a way that hasn't been done before, get out there and try it. You are not bound by the list of career opportunities I so diligently researched and listed for you. There are loads of opportunities that I either failed to mention (sorry) or that don't even exist yet. I mean, think about all the burgeoning industries we didn't even touch base on? Virtual reality, biotechnology, mother f*cking space travel for leisure! There's so much out there. You create your own destiny, so if you have a goal or an idea, don't let anybody tell you that something is impossible. Get out there and enjoy every minute of the game!

CONCLUSION

It's been quite a journey taking you on a tour of the opportunities this ever-changing world has to offer. I've done my best to inspire as many options as possible in a no-bullshit way that I wish someone had done for me when I was first entering the workforce. Why sugarcoat it? You deserve to know what you are getting into.

There is an endless world out there full of opportunities. You can work in healthcare or become a coding digital nomad. You can become a Microinfluencer or a trade school plumber. You can get a PhD in biomechanics or take MOOCs on UX Design. Only you can decide what road you want to take. Keep learning, stay on your own path, and don't listen to the naysayers! Oh, and do your best to stay out of debt... Debt is one of the fastest ways to shrink your list of opportunities (not to say you can't swim your way out of debt and come out on top).

I challenge you to start your journey today. Research a career that interests you. Sign up for a class or webinar. Even if you are insanely overwhelmed and just need to flesh it out and journal, that is a fabulous first step!

If you embark on a career path and find it's not the right fit, or if the market shifts and your job becomes less in demand, remember our discussions. There's no such thing as failure, only opportunities for growth and learning. You possess the resilience and adaptability to navigate these challenges. You're not destined for a life on autopilot, toiling away in a dead-end job. You're meant for change, for purpose. Embrace it.

Have a balanced and healthy life, keep chasing your purpose, whatever that may be, and do not get discouraged. The constant mystery and change are exciting. Keep your head high and keep going even when it gets tough.

Remember, you're never alone on this journey. Don't hesitate to reach out when you need support. Ask questions, seek guidance. Surround yourself with a community of like-minded individuals, all striving for success. Share your experiences, your triumphs, and your challenges. Your journey is not meant to be solitary. Learn from others, and let them learn from you. Together, we can achieve more.

It's truly been a rewarding and emotional journey writing this book for you. I hope you can close this book with an ambitious spirit ready to take on the road.

Sleep well, eat well, keep moving, connect with others, and, for f*cksake, shut out the naysayers. You are a badass, and you deserve to live like one. Now, get out there and spin that wheel!

SPREAD THE LOVE: LEAVE A REVIEW

First off, high-five for finishing "Career Roulette: Navigating the Chaotic Journey of Modern Adulting"! We hope it brought some laughs, a few "aha" moments, and plenty of useful advice to your career journey.

HELP US OUT, PRETTY PLEASE?

If you enjoyed the book we'd love it if you could leave a review on Amazon. Think of it as your good deed for the day—plus, you'll get some good karma points.

HOW TO LEAVE A REVIEW (IT'S EASIER THAN DECIDING WHAT TO WATCH ON NETFLIX):

1. **Visit the Amazon Product Page**: Click your way over to the book's page on Amazon.

2. Log In: Make sure you're logged into your Amazon account (no lurking in the shadows!).

3. Rate and Review: Smash that "Write a customer review" button. Give it some stars (5 is my favorite number, but no pressure) and tell the world what you think.

4. Submit: Hit "Submit" and do a little happy dance. You've just made our day!

NEED SOME INSPIRATION? HERE'S WHAT TO INCLUDE:

- **What You Loved**: What made you laugh, cry, or go "Hmm, that's interesting!"
- **Golden Nuggets**: Share any advice or tips that rocked your world.
- **Personal Wins**: How did the book help you in your career chaos?

WHY BOTHER?

Your review helps other readers decide if our book is worth their precious time. Plus, it makes us feel all warm and fuzzy inside. Whether you write a novel or just a quick line, we appreciate every word!

THANKS A MILLION!

You're the best! Thanks for taking a few minutes to spread the love. May your career journey be epic and your coffee always be strong.

SPREAD THE LOVE: LEAVE A REVIEW

Cheers,

J.T. Paige

Scan here for quick access to Amazon page

BIBLIOGRAPHY

10 Inspiring Career Change Success Stories - UNMUDL. (n.d.). https://unmudl.com/blog/inspiring-career-change-success-stories

12 Ways to Live More Sustainably. (n.d.). https://www.biologicaldiversity.org/programs/population_and_sustainability/sustainability/live_more_sustainably.html

Aristotle's Rhetoric (Stanford Encyclopedia of Philosophy). (2022, March 15). https://plato.stanford.edu/entries/aristotle-rhetoric/#:~:text=The%20methodical%20core%20of%20Aristotle's,the%20argument%20(logos)%20itself.

Ayoola, E. (2024, May 8). *The best budget apps for 2024.* NerdWallet. https://www.nerdwallet.com/article/finance/best-budget-apps

Basu, T. (2024, February 12). *How to build a personal Brand (Complete guide).* Thinkific. https://www.thinkific.com/blog/personal-branding-guide/

Beck, J. S. (2020). *Cognitive Behavior Therapy: Basics and Beyond.* Guilford Publications.

Bentley, J. (2023, July 7). What are the Benefits of Teaching English Abroad? *ITA Blog.* https://www.internationalteflacademy.com/blog/benefits-of-teaching-english-abroad

Berger, S. (2019, April 1). Oprah Winfrey: This is the moment my "job ended" and my "calling began." *CNBC.* https://www.cnbc.com/2019/04/01/how-oprah-winfrey-found-her-calling.html

Bose, I. (2024, March 29). 17 Impactful Persuasive Techniques to become a Master Public Speaker. *The Learning Hub | Eventible.* https://www.eventible.com/learning/persuasive-techniques/#:~:text=Persuasive%20techniques%20in%20public%20speaking,credibility%20and%20convey%20their%20message.

Brower, T., PhD. (2022, March 29). Know When to Say No: 3 Ways Saying No Can Build Your career. *Forbes.* https://www.forbes.com/sites/tracybrower/2022/03/27/know-when-to-say-no-3-ways-saying-no-can-build-your-career/?sh=1bb2614252e8

Burnette, M. (2024a, February 8). *How much should I have in savings?* NerdWallet. https://www.nerdwallet.com/article/banking/how-much-should-i-have-in-savings#:~:text=For%20savings%2C%20aim%20to%20keep,benefi-cial%20in%20a%20financial%20emergency.

Burnette, M. (2024b, May 9). *Best High-Yield Savings Accounts of May 2024 (Up to 5.27%) - NerdWallet*. NerdWallet. https://www.nerdwallet.com/best/banking/high-yield-online-savings-accounts

Burr, B. (n.d.). *Monday Morning Podcast*. All Things Comedy Network.

Chamberlain, E. (n.d.). *Anything Goes*. Ramble.

Coach, C. N. J. S. H. S. (2024, March 19). *Mastering time management for your side hustle in 7 simple steps*. https://www.linkedin.com/pulse/mastering-time-management-your-side-hustle-7-simple-christen-n--gol0c/

Conn, L. (2024, May 2). Why the internship needs a rebrand. *Forbes*. https://www.forbes.com/sites/lisaconn/2024/04/30/the-internship-is-dead-long-live-the-internship/?sh=1cf8379c7c51

Cruze, R. (2024, April 23). *How to change your money mindset*. Ramsey Solutions. https://www.ramseysolutions.com/budgeting/understanding-your-money-mindset

Cultural competence: an important skill set for the 21st century. (n.d.). https://extensionpublications.unl.edu/assets/html/g1375/build/g1375.htm

Cunff, A. L. (2020, August 9). *Mindful productivity: a sustainable way to work and think*. Ness Labs. https://nesslabs.com/mindful-productivity-2

Darrohn, S. (2023, September 12). 5 Digital Marketing trends to expect in 2023. *Forbes*. https://www.forbes.com/sites/forbesagencycouncil/2023/03/31/5-digital-marketing-trends-to-expect-in-2023

Digital Skills Assessment Tool. (n.d.). https://europa.eu/europass/digitalskills/screen/home

Discover thousands of collaborative articles on 2500+ skills. (n.d.). https://www.linkedin.com/pulse/networking-tech-strategies-building-your-professional-ashimi/

Eitel, B. (2023, July 6). *7 tips to manage your identity and protect your privacy online*. National Cybersecurity Alliance. https://staysafeonline.org/resources/7-tips-to-manage-your-identity/

Ellevate. (2020, July 23). Millennials want a healthy Work-Life balance. Here's what bosses can do. *Forbes*. https://www.forbes.com/sites/ellevate/2020/07/23/millennials-want-a-healthy-work-life-balance-heres-what-bosses-can-do/

Ellingrud, K., Sanghvi, S., Dandona, G. S., Madgavkar, A., Chui, M., White, O., &

Hasebe, P. (2023). Generative AI and the future of work in America. In *McKinsey & Company*. https://www.mckinsey.com/mgi/our-research/generative-ai-and-the-future-of-work-in-america

Entrepreneurial Mindset: What is It & How to Think Like an Entrepreneur. (n.d.). https://www.betterup.com/blog/entrepreneurship-mindset

Falconer, J., & Falconer, J. (2022, April 27). *Why Learn to Code? 17 Benefits of Learning to Code*. SitePoint. https://www.sitepoint.com/why-learn-to-code/

Farran, P. (2020, April 25). *"Work/Life Balance" is an ill-conceived notion*. https://www.linkedin.com/pulse/worklife-balance-ill-conceived-notion-patrick-farran/

Fear of public speaking: How can I overcome it? (2017, May 17). Mayo Clinic. https://www.mayoclinic.org/diseases-conditions/specific-phobias/expert-answers/fear-of-public-speaking/faq-20058416

Federal Student Aid. (n.d.-a). https://studentaid.gov/debt-relief-announcement

Federal Student Aid. (n.d.-b). https://studentaid.gov/manage-loans/forgiveness-cancellation/public-service

Fellow.App. (2023, January 17). *What is the Importance of Lifelong Learning in Career Development?* Fellow.app. https://fellow.app/blog/productivity/what-is-the-importance-of-lifelong-learning-in-career-development/

Finneran, K. (2024, February 20). *The top social media and digital marketing trends to watch in 2024*. Forbes. https://www.forbes.com/sites/katyfinneran/2023/12/21/the-top-social-media-and-digital-marketing-trends-to-watch-in-2024/?sh=4cbea6a42f17

Freelancers Union. (2024, March 21). *Home - Freelancers Union*. https://freelancersunion.org/

Gershman, S. (2021, September 17). *To overcome your fear of public speaking, stop thinking about yourself*. Harvard Business Review. https://hbr.org/2019/09/to-overcome-your-fear-of-public-speaking-stop-thinking-about-yourself

Gillett, R. (2015, October 6). 21 highly successful people who rebounded after getting fired. *Business Insider*. https://www.businessinsider.com/successful-people-who-were-fired-2015-10#a-baltimore-tv-producer-told-oprah-winfrey-she-was-unfit-for-television-news-16

Gillihan, S. J. (2020). *Cognitive Behavioural therapy made simple: 10 Strategies for Managing Anxiety, Depression, Anger, Panic and Worry*. Hachette UK.

H, B. (2023, March 5). Beat Procrastination with the Nothing Alternative - Ben H - Medium. *Medium*. https://giraffemindset.medium.com/beat-procrastination-with-the-nothing-alternative-7b60a5b813b6#:~:text=Well%2C%20according%20to%20Raymond%20Chandler,you're%20supposed%20to%20do.

Hendry, E. R. (2013, December 4). 7 Epic fails brought to you by the genius mind of Thomas Edison. *Smithsonian Magazine*. https://www.smithsonianmag.com/innovation/7-epic-fails-brought-to-you-by-the-genius-mind-of-thomas-edison-180947786/

How to become a digital nomad in 2023: Steps & expert tips. (2024, April 18). Pumble Learn. https://pumble.com/learn/digital-nomad-visa/how-to-become-digital-nomad/

How to break the mental health stigma in the workplace. (2023, July 3). HSI. https://hsi.com/blog/how-to-break-the-mental-health-stigma-in-the-workplace

How to build a coding portfolio | BestColleges. (n.d.). BestColleges.com. https://www.bestcolleges.com/bootcamps/guides/how-to-build-coding-portfolio/#:

How to make a budget | Budgeting for Beginners | Erin Condren. (n.d.). https://www.erincondren.com/inspiration-center-how-to-budget

How to write SEO content: 8 quality tips and techniques | Upwork. (n.d.). https://www.upwork.com/resources/how-to-write-seo-content

Indeed Editorial Team. (2022, June 24). *10 Ideation Techniques for Problem-Solving*. Indeed.com. https://www.indeed.com/career-advice/career-development/ideation-techniques

Indeed Editorial Team. (2023a, February 3). *Trade School vs. College: Key Differences and Benefits of Each*. Indeed.com. https://www.indeed.com/career-advice/career-development/trade-school-vs-college

Indeed Editorial Team. (2023b, September 15). *9 Effective Business Networking Tips For Young Professionals*. Indeed.com. https://in.indeed.com/career-advice/career-development/business-networking-tips

Internships Abroad | GoAbroad.com. (n.d.). GoAbroad.com. https://www.goabroad.com/intern-abroad

Jayakumar, A. (2024, April 26). *What is debt consolidation, and should I consolidate?* NerdWallet. https://www.nerdwallet.com/article/finance/consolidate-debt

Jeppsson, C. (2019, April 3). How I landed a full stack developer job without a tech degree or work experience. *Medium*. https://medium.com/free-code-camp/how-i-landed-a-full-stack-developer-job-without-a-tech-degree-or-work-experience-6add97be2051

Job burnout: How to spot it and take action. (2023, November 30). Mayo Clinic. https://www.mayoclinic.org/healthy-lifestyle/adult-health/in-depth/burnout/art-

BIBLIOGRAPHY

20046642

Jpotyraj. (2021, July 9). *What is Coding– 5 Key Advantages of Learning To Code.* Berkeley Boot Camps. https://bootcamp.berkeley.edu/blog/what-is-coding-key-advantages/

Justin. (2024, April 16). *Take a mental health test.* Mental Health America. https://screening.mhanational.org/screening-tools/

Kashyap, A. (2023, February 17). *Impact of peer pressure on career choices.* https://www.linkedin.com/pulse/impact-peer-pressure-career-choices-prof-anil-kashyap#:~:text=Young%20people%20are%20more%20prone,one%20that%20suits%20them%20best.

Kopp, C. M. (2023, August 7). *How to get paid to go to school.* Investopedia. https://www.investopedia.com/articles/budgeting-savings/090316/how-get-paid-go-school.asp

Kruse, K. (2024, February 20). *The 80/20 rule and how it can change your life.* Forbes. https://www.forbes.com/sites/kevinkruse/2016/03/07/80-20-rule/?sh=70ba97fd3814

Lapointe, G. (2023, October 19). *8 of the Most Violent, Original Endings of Classic Fairy Tales.* BOOK RIOT. https://bookriot.com/original-fairy-tale-endings/

Law, T. J. (2021, February 15). Bootstrapping a Business: A Guide to Success. *Oberlo.* https://www.oberlo.com/blog/bootstrapping-a-business

Leikvoll, V. (2023, October 23). *A Guide to 10 of the Fastest-Growing Industries to Watch in 2023.* Leaders.com. https://leaders.com/articles/business/fastest-growing-industries/

Lundia, S. (2023, May 12). 10 Innovative Strategies for bootstrapped startup marketing on a Budget. *Forbes.* https://www.forbes.com/sites/forbesbusinesscouncil/2023/05/11/10-innovative-strategies-for-bootstrapped-startup-marketing-on-a-budget/

Marr, B. (2024, May 9). The 10 Most In-Demand Skills in 2024. *Forbes.* https://www.forbes.com/sites/bernardmarr/2023/11/27/the-10-most-in-demand-skills-in-2024/

Martin, M. (2023, October 23). *Conducting a personal SWOT analysis to chart your future.* Business News Daily. https://www.businessnewsdaily.com/5543-personal-swot-analysis.html

Mental Health and Personality Tests. (n.d.). Psychology Today. https://www.psychologytoday.com/us/tests

Mindfulness meditation: A research-proven way to reduce stress. (2019, October

30). *https://www.apa.org.* https://www.apa.org/topics/mindfulness/meditation#:~:text=By%20lowering%20the%20stress%20response,with%20attention%20and%20emotion%20regulation.

MindTools | Home. (n.d.). https://www.mindtools.com/ao2rt8j/scamper

Mishra, A. (2023, September 5). *Mastering Effective learning on online platforms: a guide to Coursera, Udemy, LinkedIn Learning, and Internshala.* https://www.linkedin.com/pulse/mastering-effective-learning-online-platforms-guide-coursera-mishra

Moran, A. (2021, October 22). *8 Unexpected Challenges that Teachers Face Abroad.* Go Overseas. https://www.gooverseas.com/blog/8-unexpected-hurdles-teachers-face-abroad

Murchison, C. (2024, February 8). *The pros & cons of taking a gap year.* Go Overseas. https://www.gooverseas.com/blog/pros-and-cons-taking-gap-year

Murphy, R. (2024, May 2). Best Budgeting apps of May 2024. *Forbes Advisor.* https://www.forbes.com/advisor/banking/best-budgeting-apps/

Navone, E. C. (2024, January 11). *Python Code Example Handbook – Sample script coding tutorial for beginners.* freeCodeCamp.org. https://www.freecodecamp.org/news/python-code-examples-sample-script-coding-tutorial-for-beginners/

Novotney, A. (n.d.). *The science of creativity.* https://www.apa.org. https://www.apa.org/gradpsych/2009/01/creativity#:~:text=Despite%20the%20widely%20held%20belief,something%20that%20anyone%20can%20cultivate.

Ollier-Malaterre, A. (2015, March 26). *How to separate the personal and professional on social media.* Harvard Business Review. https://hbr.org/2015/03/how-to-separate-the-personal-and-professional-on-social-media

Ong, S. Q. (2023, October 25). *23 Beginner Blogging Tips to Get Better at Blogging (Fast).* SEO Blog by Ahrefs. https://ahrefs.com/blog/blogging-tips/

Piccardo, R. (2021, August 26). *Want to turn your passion project into a successful business? Try these 7 tips from people who have done it.* The Muse. https://www.themuse.com/advice/how-to-turn-passion-project-into-business

Potter, D. (2019, May 31). *How to Say No: A guide to saying no politely | Grammarly.* How to Say No: A Guide to Saying No Politely | Grammarly. https://www.grammarly.com/blog/saying-no/

Raypole, C. (2023, March 10). *Cognitive behavioral therapy: What is it and how does it work?* Healthline. https://www.healthline.com/health/cognitive-behavioral-therapy

Rizvi, J. (2024, March 12). Sustainability has gone mainstream across industries.

Forbes. https://www.forbes.com/sites/jiawertz/2024/03/09/sustainability-has-gone-mainstream-across-industries/?sh=1f4d0d1ba7bd

Rolfe, R. (2023, September 20). *The best coding Languages to learn for Beginners - National Coding Week.* National Coding Week. https://codingweek.org/the-best-coding-languages-to-learn-for-beginners/

Ryan, K. (2023, December 29). *The 5 Best Budgeting Apps to Make Managing Your Money Easier in 2024.* Buy Side From WSJ. https://www.wsj.com/buyside/personal-finance/best-budgeting-apps-01656001549

Sauer, M. (2024, February 26). 55-year-old whose backyard side hustle brought in nearly $20,000 in a month: 'Anyone can do this.' *CNBC.* https://www.cnbc.com/2023/09/30/55-year-old-with-lucrative-backyard-side-hustle-anyone-can-do-this.html

Schaffner, A. K., PhD. (2024, March 11). *How to Overcome Fear of Failure: Your Ultimate guide.* PositivePsychology.com. https://positivepsychology.com/fear-of-failure/

Schooley, S. (2024, January 3). *What is a SWOT Analysis? (And When To Use It).* Business News Daily. https://www.businessnewsdaily.com/4245-swot-analysis.html

Scotch. (n.d.). *Buffett's two lists.* https://modelthinkers.com/mental-model/buffetts-two-lists#:~:text=Buffett's%20Two%20Lists%20is%20a,anything%20on%20the%20remaining%2020.

Sellas, B. B. (2023, April 7). *How to use social media for professional networking.* https://www.linkedin.com/pulse/how-use-social-media-professional-networking-brooke-b-sellas/

Signs-Your-Workplace-May-Be-Impacting-Your-Mental-Health. (n.d.). https://www.texashealth.org/areyouawellbeing/Behavioral-Health/Signs-Your-Workplace-May-Be-Impacting-Your-Mental-Health

Smith, J. (2023, December 14). What are the Basic Requirements to Teach English Abroad? *ITA Blog.* https://www.internationalteflacademy.com/blog/basic-requirements-to-teach-english-abroad

Spotify. (n.d.). https://open.spotify.com/episode/0wwhKtpF9RcxbLTGAt2nAe?si=9a08dd71c6634590

Staff, C. (2024, January 5). *10 tips to improve your public speaking skills.* Coursera. https://www.coursera.org/articles/public-speaking

Study Abroad Programs & Internships | IES Abroad. (2024, January 31). IES Abroad. https://www.iesabroad.org/

SWOT Analysis Template Spreadsheet. (n.d.). [Software]. https://images.business

newsdaily.com/app/uploads/2019/06/14132541/S.W.O.T.-Analysis-Matrix-Template.xlsx

The Artist's Way: 30th Anniversary Edition: Cameron, Julia: 9780143129257: Amazon.com: Books. (n.d.). My Book

The difference between federal and private student loans. (n.d.). Sallie Mae. https://www.salliemae.com/college-planning/student-loans-and-borrowing/compare-federal-vs-private-loans/#:~:text=When%20comparing%20federal%20loans%20vs,process%2C%20and%20terms%20and%20conditions.

UOTP Marketing. (2024, January 12). 15 Benefits of online education: Advantages of online learning. *University of the Potomac.* https://potomac.edu/benefits-of-online-education/

U.S. Bureau of Labor Statistics. (2022, April). *Green Growth: Employment projections in environmentally focused occupations.* Career Outlook. https://www.bls.gov/careeroutlook/2022/data-on-display/green-growth.htm

Venchiarutti, B. (2023, November 5). *A guide to preventing burnout in your 20s — The Twenties Detox.* The Twenties Detox. https://www.thetwentiesdetox.com/journal/a-guide-to-preventing-burnout-in-your-20s

Walden University. (2022, October 22). How to choose online classes—5 tips to help. *Walden University.* https://www.waldenu.edu/programs/resource/how-to-choose-online-classes-5-tips-to-help

What is Analysis Paralysis? 9 Tips to Overcome It. (n.d.). https://www.betterup.com/blog/analysis-paralysis

Wikipedia contributors. (2003, August 11). *SWOT analysis.* Wikipedia. https://en.wikipedia.org/wiki/SWOT_analysis#:~:text=One%20way%20of%20using%20SWOT,is%20to%20find%20new%20markets.

Wilds, J. (2023, October 2). *The importance of digital literacy in the modern workplace.* https://www.linkedin.com/pulse/importance-digital-literacy-modern-workplace-jemelle-wilds

Wissman, B. (2017, November 27). 10 Strategies for Entrepreneurs Dealing with Failure. *Entrepreneur.* https://www.entrepreneur.com/leadership/10-strategies-for-entrepreneurs-dealing-with-failure/304948

Printed in Great Britain
by Amazon